DRIFT BOAT STRATEGIES

DRIFT BOAT STRATEGIES
ROWING & FISHING SKILLS FOR THE WESTERN ANGLER

Neale Streeks

Illustrations by Rod Walinchus

PRUETT PUBLISHING COMPANY
BOULDER, COLORADO

Printed in the United States

10 9 8 7 6 5 4 3 2 1

Library of Congress Cataloging-in-Publication data

Streeks, Neale.
    Driftboat strategies : rowing & fishing skills for the western angler / Neale Streeks ; illustrations by Rod Walinchus.
        p.   cm.
    Includes index.
    ISBN 0-87108-887-8 (pb)
    1. Fly fishing—West (U.S.) 2. Drift boats—West (U.S.)
I. Title.
SH456.S834   1998
799.1'757'0978—dc21   97-35350
                                                            CIP

COVER AND BOOK DESIGN BY JULIE NOYES LONG
BOOK COMPOSITION BY LYN CHAFFEE
COVER AND INTERIOR PHOTOGRAPHS BY NEALE STREEKS
ILLUSTRATIONS BY ROD WALINCHUS

Warning: River boating is a potentially dangerous, high-risk activity. The information presented here has been compiled by an experienced drift boat operator, but the book is not a substitute for the reader's own judgment and personal responsibility. You alone are responsible for your safety. Come to the activity prepared: Bring the proper equipment, experience, and common sense. Recreate wisely and safely.

CONTENTS

INTRODUCTION

1. BASIC ROWING SKILLS............5

THE BASIC OAR STROKE............5
THE BASIC ROWING STROKE............12
ANTICIPATING THE RIVER............17
BASIC MANEUVERING............20

2. THE CRAWL STROKE

3. UNDERSTANDING MOVING WATER: RIVER HAZARDS AND
HOW TO AVOID THEM............50

WRAPPING BOULDERS AND FLIPPING IN HOLES............51
LEDGES AND DIVERSION DAMS............66
LOGJAMS............67
RIVER BENDS............70
READING AND CLEARING RAPIDS............73
WHIRLPOOLS............83
EFFECTS OF THE ELEMENTS............85
MANMADE HAZARDS............89

4. FLOAT-FISHING STRATEGIES: IMPROVING YOUR CATCH
RATE............92

THINKING LIKE A TROUT............92
ROWING A CASTING PLATFORM............106

5. FLY FISHING FROM A BOAT: STRATEGIES FOR SAFE AND
CONTROLLED CASTING............115

SPECIAL CASTING TECHNIQUES............117
FLOAT-FISHING TACKLE............124

6. CHOOSING AND OUTFITTING THE RIGHT BOAT............*126*

RAFT, PRAM, OR DRIFT BOAT?............126
ALUMINUM, FIBERGLASS, OR WOOD?: DRIFT
  BOAT AND PRAM CONSTRUCTION OPTIONS............138
RIGGING THE CRAFT............145

**7. EXPEDITION RIGGING: GEARING UP FOR A MULTIDAY
FLOAT TRIP**............*155*

FLOAT-FISHING CHECKLISTS............163

8. TRAILERING, RAMP USE, AND RIVER ETIQUETTE............*170*

NEGOTIATING RAMPS............172

CONCLUSION............*175*
**APPENDIX: HATCHES AND FLY PATTERNS FOR FLY FISHING
WESTERN RIVERS**............*178*
INDEX............*198*

INTRODUCTION

*F*loat-fishing a river can be one of life's great pleasures. There is a special charm in pushing off into clear currents and watching spectacular landscapes sweep by. The sound of water lapping on the hull, and scents of clean air, earth, forest, and stream can intoxicate the senses. There are pine and cottonwood groves to float through, massive mountain ranges to lead the way, drinking wildlife to be quietly observed, and clouds dressed in warm sunset pastels racing across the big western sky. Sun and breeze burnish your skin. Your whole being comes vibrantly alive. It's easy to become a river addict!

A deeper element is added when one is also targeting trout, for now the water's character, fish behavior, insect hatches, and other phenomena of the river world must be understood if a float fisherman is to do his best. There are the mechanical aspects of rowing to be learned and mastered, plus the accumulation of knowledge about river life and game fish. There is no aspect of a river valley that doesn't somehow come into play in a float fisher's pursuit of the quarry.

Drift boat fly fishing, and floating rivers in general, has boomed in popularity over the last twenty years. For many who take up the sport, a hit and miss approach is undertaken. Once they obtain the craft (which can be quite expensive these days), no effort is spent in learning much about its use, they figure they'll just float the river, taking it as it comes. It's common to see novice floaters bouncing off boulders, spinning out of control, and taking the "pinball" route down more challenging runs. Not only does this endanger those in the boat and ruin fishing opportunities, it often violates the rights of other

Pushing off for a day's fishing. Expectations are never higher!

river users. A definite lack of courtesy and competence on the part of many float fishers has been a noticeable part of float fishing's continuing growth. In addition, numerous drownings occur every year, mostly among novices who lack knowledge of moving water and its powerful, unforgiving qualities. Boats are lost or ruined, too, substantial investments gone literally down the drain.

When fly fishing from an oar-powered craft, whether a raft, drift boat, or pram, a change in fishing technique must be adopted if fly fishers want to fully capitalize on the new opportunities that come their way. As a full-time fly-fishing guide, I get to see how many fly fishers who go on guided trips fail to recognize this fact. New approaches must be learned that are different from those relied upon by most wade fishers. These new approaches aren't difficult, in fact they're easy, but without adopting them, fishing success will never be maximized. A novice rower floating (or bouncing) down a river with a fly fisher, neither of whom understand float fishing's special demands, is likely to be a poor fishing team indeed!

This book covers the basic mechanics of rowing, reading rivers, and fishing, and it provides information on how to select boats and rig boats for extended expedition-style trips. Not all boats are suited for all rivers. White-water rivers have different demands than more placid ones that get a lot of wind. There are also rivers that offer multiday float-fishing adventure with streamside camping along the way. These are among the world's most beautiful float trips. We'll look at the equipment and skills needed for these, too.

It's been my goal to touch upon every aspect of river float-fishing that a novice would need to understand, information gleaned from twenty years as a river guide. I hope to cover it in enough detail that intermediate-level floaters will get a lot out of it as well. Once these skills become second nature, your enjoyment of rivers will increase all the more. For example, a tree may be just a tree to the average bystander. To the attentive float fisher, it might be casting shadows along a bank that is where trout fin in summer's heat. Its root system could be propping up an undercut bank where a particularly fine specimen resides. If it falls in the water, eroded out by seasonal ice jams and a river heavy with snowmelt, it could choke a channel and become a serious navigational hazard.

A swallow might be just another bird to some. To the riverborne angler it's a wondrous creature just returned perhaps from the depths of Brazil to feast on the *Baetis* mayfly hatch, which begins in central Montana around April 14 every year. It is surely no coincidence that both show up about the same time. Thousands of years of evolution have established river patterns, some of which no doubt have gone undiscovered by the individual and humanity as a whole.

This same *Baetis* mayfly, which seems so small and insignificant at first glance, not only feeds swallows from South America but also brings trout to the surface and to knowledgeable fly fishers: "Let's be at Pelican Islands at 2 P.M. for the *Baetis* hatch." What a bug! Those in the know not only row well but understand where and when to look for the most alluring trout action. Yes, rivers are all motion and change. Their wanderings and life-forms take a lifetime to understand.

When anglers try to fish from a drift boat, the rower's knowledge and skill can count most in the making of a great day. For not only will he get his party to their destination safely and on time, but he will also have maximized the fishing potential by slowing the craft down to take advantage of optimal casting distances!

Safety is paramount, of course. Floating rivers involves risks, dangers that seem to arise so quickly that any hesitation in decision making and follow-through can be injurious to life and property, and even fatal. Human nature often leads the unlearned and inexperienced to do the exact opposite of what should be done, facilitating disaster instead of averting it. River knowledge doesn't come naturally—it has to be learned.

The object of this book, then, is to provide a solid base of information for novices to intermediate-level float fishermen, a base that will help them understand moving water, use the proper rowing skills to avert danger, and provide ideas to increase fish catch rates. It's a lot easier to absorb the float-fishing skills this book provides than it is to spend years in hit or miss experimentation trying to figure them out!

Even those who are not into fishing might enjoy learning more about rowing and river life. The more one understands the infinite intricacies of water and stone, algae and aspen, insect, fish, mammal, and bird, the more lasting enjoyment he or she may reap. Rowing is great aerobic exercise too, and the surroundings are much more appealing than some sweat-soaked gym! The right boat, the right oar stroke, a well cast fly—there are few simple pleasures so great as that perfect day rowing downstream.

1

BASIC ROWING SKILLS

*R*owing seems almost as much a part of human nature as walking to me. To the ancients of many cultures it was a prime mode of transportation. Some may have rowed for fun but others were slaves, rowing for commerce and war. Although rowing under such circumstances surely held no novelty, rowing for sport and recreation is exhilarating. Pulling on oars, increasing the heart rate, listening to and feeling the water's currents, all enrich life. The effects are immediate, thus gratifying. Views from the river are always of interest. And I can escape the grimy crust of urban concrete realities one day more!

The Basic Oar Stroke

Rowing is a fairly basic physical action, yet there are subtleties to consider. Oars can be mechanically fixed at the oar locks or spin free for ultimate hand control. There are adaptations and manipulations you may never have thought of. There's the lazy pace of slow, open water, and the vigorous demands and split-second decision making of tough white water. As with most sports, rowing becomes somewhat of an art in its extreme applications. Because our purpose is primarily fishing, the emphasis is on smooth control to maximize the angler's casting advantage. It's not a power stroke that's usually needed but one that incorporates finesse with good timing. We'll begin with the basics, then gradually expand our horizons until all river navigation and fishing possibilities are explored.

The rowing's easy here, but what's around the next bend?

HAND POSITION

The hands are placed over the oar handles in a natural fashion, so that the rower is looking at the backs of his hands. The thumbs can be placed over the ends of the oar handles or wrapped underneath. The oar and oar lock design now come into play, as do the oars' position in regard to the locks.

Let's take a moment to look at oar and oar lock designs, because they do affect the hands' duties at the oars.

HORN OAR LOCKS, OARS WITH STOPPERS

At one time this was probably the most common oar lock arrangement and is still used widely. I use them on my drift boat, with epoxied rope tightly wound over a length of the oar to keep it from popping out through the horn. On the handle end of this rope-wound segment is a rubber stopper. This keeps the oars at the right length for rowing while also stopping them from sliding out through the horns and into the river when I let go of them.

With this arrangement, the hands must keep the oar blades at the correct rowing angle in the river. The proper blade angle varies from being perpendicular to the water to slightly tilted to the rear,

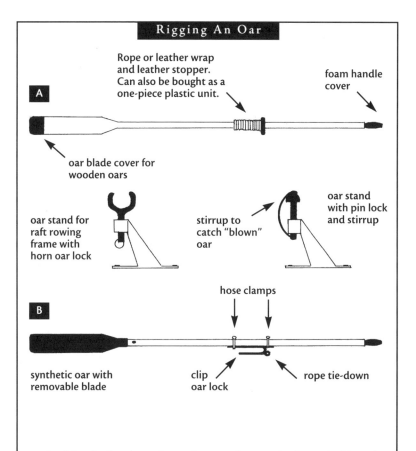

Rigging An Oar

A

Rope or leather wrap and leather stopper. Can also be bought as a one-piece plastic unit.

foam handle cover

oar blade cover for wooden oars

oar stand for raft rowing frame with horn oar lock

stirrup to catch "blown" oar

oar stand with pin lock and stirrup

B

hose clamps

synthetic oar with removable blade

clip oar lock

rope tie-down

A. Traditionally rigged oars featured wraps of rope or leather to build up the thickness of the oar diameter so the oar wouldn't pop out of the horn oar lock. A rubber oar stop was then secured to keep the oar from slipping out of the horn. Proper oar-blade angle is maintained by the rower's grip.

B. Clip oar locks have been popular on big white-water rivers. These slip over a pin. This keeps the oar blade at the proper rowing angle and allows the oar to pop free should it hit a rock under extreme water pressure.

with the top of the blade tilted back up to 20 degrees or so beyond the perpendicular. The angle of the oar blade has to do with the direction you're pushing the water during the strongest part of the stroke. The blade angle can be rolled or changed to do other things, too, such as feathering, to brake gently, and ruddering and sweeping while pointed toward the bow. (We'll examine these techniques later.)

In any case, your grip on the oar must be firm enough to maintain the correct blade angle. Beginners will have to look at the oar blades frequently to check the angle. You'll know you're way off if you make a power stroke and almost fall backward off your seat! This happens when the blades are accidentally spun to a horizontal position that is parallel with the river's surface. There will be no water resistance, and because you're used to leaning on the oars for support when they're held at the proper angle during an oar stroke, you will fall back. Experienced rowers can tell the oar-blade angle by feel.

There are several oar-lock designs that eliminate the need to hold the oar blade at the right angle manually. Many experienced boatmen and most beginners prefer these alternatives. It is a little disconcerting for beginners to row like mad to miss a hazard, to find both oar blades at ineffective horizontal angles! Once the oar blade is locked in to a good rowing angle, you can loosen your grip and give blade angle no more immediate thought. The following are fixed-blade-position alternatives.

Horns and Oars with Oar Right Stopper

This simple gadget is secured to the oar in place of a traditional stopper. The Oar Right attachment fills in the space in the horn, thus keeping the oar from spinning. The blade angle is locked in place with only a tiny bit of rotation possible. This is a good, inexpensive option for beginning rowers.

Pins and Clips

This is a more unusual-looking arrangement, and is commonly used on whitewater rafts. A clip is hose-clamped onto the oar. Its specialized design allows it to be jammed onto the pin, which is attached to the rowing frame in place of a horn oar lock. This locks the oar blade firmly in at a good rowing angle that can be changed only by

The Oar Right oar stopper keeps the oar-blade angle locked in place for easier rowing.

loosening the hose clamps on the oar and clip, rotating the oar by the blade, and retightening the hose clamps.

The other important feature of pins and clips is that they allow the oar to pop free from the pin should the oar slam into a rock or cliff wall, a situation in which it might otherwise break. (Horn oarlocks allow this, too.) This is a common occurrence in running white water. Originally boatmen tied in their oars, and many still do, because once the oar clip blows off the pin, the oar can easily fall overboard. The force of impact and danger of capsizing diminish one's chances of holding on to a loose 10-foot oar in raging water.

A more recent alternative to tying in the oars are oar stirrups. These lasso an oar that blows off a pin until the boatman can reposition himself at his seat and grab it again. On big-water expeditions of several days, it's wise both to tie in your oars (and all your other equipment) and use stirrups. At least one spare oar should always be taken, too.

Pins and clips are seen on some fishing boats, but the less cumbersome and cheaper Oar Right stoppers have largely taken their place on mellower trout rivers.

Regardless of oar-lock design, one must consider how closely together the oar handles are positioned when oars are measured and set up. (The stopper or pin and clip position becomes, for all practical purposes, permanent while rowing, though most can be changed.) Most people like to leave just a few inches between their oar handles when they're extended out all the way and held horizontally. If they're any closer, it's easy to pinch or crush your thumbs between them when rowing. There are a few boatmen who actually like to overlap their oar handles and row in a circular or offset motion, with one hand going over the other to avoid finger-crushing collisions. The idea here is to gain leverage, for the longer the part of the oar on the rower's side of the oar lock (within reason), the more powerful the rowing leverage. This overlapping-oar technique is best left to the experienced, for the "education through pain" of occasionally smashing your fingers until habituated to the style is no great fun.

You'll often see boats rigged with the oars going to the opposite extreme—that of being too far apart. This is often done as an oversight by novice boat owners. Experienced boaters take their oar positioning seriously. What happens when you fix your oars too far apart is one, you lose leverage, and two, the weight of the oar outside the oarlock, that length of oar you pick up and swing back upstream hundreds and even thousands of times a day, is increased. Too much space between oar handles and too much oar outside the boat makes for a decidedly harder rowing day. If every time you lift the oar blade out of the water and it weighs five pounds, and you then make five thousand oar strokes a day, you've lifted an accumulated twenty-five thousand pounds! Think about it.

Only recently have oars hit the market that have adjustable weighting systems in the oar handles (after how many millennia of rowing?). You can add or subtract weight till the oars are balanced to your liking. I have long thought that an oar should automatically balance when you let go of it, with the blade lifting itself clear of the water until its shaft comes slowly to rest at the horizontal. In that way the amount of weight you've lifted with each oar stroke is significantly reduced by the end of the day. This is no small point when you're averaging ten thousand oar strokes a day!

Pins, clips, and oar stirrups are popular white-water oar arrangements. The clip is firmly attached to the oar and slides over the pin, which is mounted in place of a horn oar lock. The stirrup attaches to the pin and catches the oar should it break loose from the pin after hitting a rock.

The Basic Rowing Stroke

The simple act of lifting the oar blades out of the water, pushing the handles forward (which, with the use of the oar locks as fulcrums, swings the blades back upstream), dipping the blades in the water, then pulling smoothly on the handles until you're leaning backward just a bit is a rhythmic and relaxing routine. There are a few facets of this basic rowing stroke that warrant closer inspection. We'll look at them one step at a time.

When lifting the oars out of the water in preparation for the next oar stroke, you don't need to raise the blades more than a few inches above the water's surface. Any more is a waste of energy. The only time you might have to lift them higher is in rapids and waves, where they might have to be lifted to clear the turbulence. You might also have to raise them up to pass over boulders or logs protruding from the river. Beginners tend to lift oars too far out of the water, splash them back down, then pull them through the water too deeply.

If using a horn oar lock with a traditional stopper, you'll have to make sure the oar blades are maintained at the proper angle by using a firm grip. The act of drawing the oar blade through the water and occasionally hitting the bottom will tend to rotate it in your hands. Included in your visual wanderings, then, should be routine glances at your oar blades to see if they're at the proper angle. With a lot of experience you can tell what the oar-blade angle is by feel alone. You might even rotate the angle a bit with your wrists during the oar stroke to gain the best pushing angle throughout the oar's path. In any case, as a beginner with free-spinning oars, you'll want to take a glance at the blade angle as you swing the oars back upstream for another stroke. The use of Oar Rights or pins and clips eliminates this concern, though many experienced boatmen prefer oars that can be "feathered" and spun to meet varying situations.

After the oar blades have been swung back upstream, dip them in the water in preparation for your back-rowing pull. Dip them quietly. Remember that you're trying to sneak up on a trout, wild animals in a wild setting. They can perceive boats that are too close or too loud. Don't splash your oars down into the water.

Your oar blades should be just barely under water. Don't dig

Effective Use of Oars

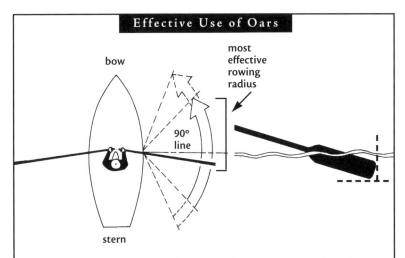

bow

most effective rowing radius

90° line

stern

The most energy-efficient part of an oar stroke is the short arc shown here as closest to the 90-degree line outside the oar lock. Experienced rowers tend to use short oar strokes that look effortless (except in demanding situations). Beginners usually make a too-wide rowing arc, which wastes a lot of energy and gains little power.

When making a back stroke, dig the oar just deep enough in the water to cover the blade. Beginners tend to dig too deeply, which dissipates leverage and oar power and can also jam the oar blade into the river bottom.

The oar-blade angle should vary from straight up and down to a slight tilt, with the top of the blade leaning back slightly toward the stern. This gives a better bite on the water as the back stroke follows through and raises the oar before it is lifted out for the next stroke.

them deeply, for that actually decreases your leverage: They are more likely to hit the bottom and will be harder to lift back up. In turbulent water, whirling subsurface currents can get such a grip on deep oars that one can barely get them back up and out of the water. This momentarily handicaps rowing, sometimes in critical situations. Keep oar strokes relatively shallow, smooth, and quiet for the best fishing.

Upon dipping your oar blades in the water, immediately begin pulling back and leaning into them. Rowing anglers usually calls for an easy but continuous pace. Slowing the boat down is every bit as important as positioning it advantageously when it comes to good fishing. It's all very rhythmic with pauses taken, though occasionally and only in slow-water, nonmaneuvering situations.

When pulling back on the oars, again, remember not to dig them overdeep, a common beginner's error. Maximize your leverage by keeping the blades just barely under the surface. You might have to observe them when learning to get the feel for the right depth, with the blade angle maintained correctly with a sure grip. Don't forget to constantly look up and ahead for river hazards, though, while also working to keep anglers ideally positioned.

Another tendency among beginners is to make too wide an oar sweep, covering too much of a semicircular path with the blade. What happens here is that an overdone oar stroke is inefficiently pushing more water perpendicular to than parallel to the boat and its intended path. This, too, is a waste of energy. It's usually easier and more effective to take three shorter strokes than two overlong ones. Experienced rowers often look like they're using very little effort and tiny little oar strokes, and such is the case. The novice will tend to over-row, dig too deep with the oars, flail them about in the air and water, and in general use way too much energy in a less than efficient fashion. There are times when you need extra power and a slightly longer oar stroke, using all the strength in your back, abdomen, legs, and arms. But practice economizing your efforts while achieving desired boat positioning and slowing.

Besides this basic oar stroke, there are variations that we'll explore later on. For in the subtleties of rowing fishermen, every possible manipulation of an oar should come into play.

BACK ROWING

The first rule of rowing, whether for fishing or in white water, is to do all your maneuvering with back strokes—by pulling on the oars, not by pushing on them. Arm, back, stomach, and leg muscles work together to make back stroking much more powerful than simply pushing the oars forward against the water. Most beginners want to push the oars forward, perhaps because they themselves are facing forward. It seems the natural thing to do at times. The biggest problem with this arises when novice rowers are faced with serious river hazards and think that they can row forward to get away from them. They usually

Back rowing—pulling back on the oars rather than pushing forward—should become a habit. It slows the boat down for better fishing and has more power for critical maneuvering.

can't. Indeed, rowing forward only increases the speed and rate with which you approach an obstacle, even when rowing down and across stream. The forward stroke is weak, generally making little progress across the current's flow and away from the obstruction. A common scenario is when beginners start off by trying to row forward to get away from a hazard, realize they can't, try to reposition (pivot) the boat, and finally begin back rowing, but all too late. Collisions in such cases are common.

The thing to do is to make back rowing a firm habit. Certainly, there are times when rowing forward is an option, usually when you're just trying to make time down a straight stretch of obstacle-free river. But any time a hazard approaches, immediately revert to back rowing. This slows the craft down and allows maximum lateral maneuverability (ferrying).

In fishing situations, you almost always want to be constantly back rowing at an easy pace to slow the boat down anyway. This allows for a much better coverage of the water with flies or lures. Consider that the boat is often out in the faster currents, whereas much of the fly placement is to slower bank waters, eddies, and to places where trout don't have to fight the full force of the current. If you do not back row, the boat whisks by all those promising pockets. Fishers can barely manage a brief, half-good presentation. There is nothing more annoying than trying to fish seriously from a drift boat that is traveling too fast and is not in the absolute best position for casting presentations. A rower who's going with the flow can be a serious irritation to those in the boat who wish to fish.

I make an oar stroke about every three seconds when guiding. I'm often rowing (not parked and wade-fishing) over eight hours a day (out of more than twelve on the river). This adds up to 1,200 oar strokes an hour, or 9,600 oar strokes a day! This is a common rowing pace for serious fishing guides. Of course, it's so habitual that it doesn't seem like that much work. I take a lot more oar strokes than footsteps in the summer! If it's been a real tough rowing day (usually due to wind or high water), my legs feel it the most at the end of the day, along with the skin on the palms of my hands. In any case, it's important to keep up a steady back-rowing pace, however intense, when rowing anglers. This soon becomes second nature, and as with any physical activity, your muscles become accustomed to it with practice, as does the skin on the palms of your hands. Many beginners choose to wear rowing gloves.

As you steadily and easily back row, you are facing forward, which is downstream. The fishers in your boat are hoping you will maintain them the proper distance from their target water, be that banks, eddy lines, rock pockets, or what have you. What's important here is to keep them a steady distance from the target water so they can fish with a fixed length of fly line. Don't let the boat drift within 10 feet of shore, then row it out 100 feet away. When hitting the banks, keep the boat a constant 50 feet or so away, or whatever distance is easy and effective for your particular fishing party. It takes constant observation and planning to keep a boat slowed down and in the perfect fishing position, for the boat is nothing more than a platform from which to cast. If your party is float-fishing and it's your turn at the oars, it's your job to position the boat conscientiously and to slow it down. This doesn't allow much break in concentration. Again, this becomes somewhat second nature with experience but always requires some thought when maintaining just the right distance from shore.

There are elements there to test and distract you, too, like side-slipping currents, power eddies, cross-winds, and rocks to be maneuvered around—not to mention beautiful scenery and wildlife to gaze at! With practice, your mind analyzes the river's flow with computer-like precision. You look to the bank every five seconds to calculate your distance from it, rhythmically continue making back strokes, plot upcoming maneuvers around obstacles, duck low casts—all in a nonstop mental and physical flow paced to match the river's cadence. Funny thing is, all this is usually quite relaxing and fun!

Anticipating the River

Skilled rowing is all in the planning. Decisions on boat positioning (the angle across the current in which the stern's pointed) and back-stroking effort need to be made in advance, before an actual hazard is physically encountered. Drift boats and rafts don't respond immediately to oar strokes. It takes several strokes to start building some inertia and speed. This inertia carries on a bit after you stop rowing, too. Over-rowing sees beginners make too many oar strokes to miss an obstacle, with the resulting momentum carrying them much farther aside than they meant to go, even running them into the bank or another hazard.

If you see a boulder coming, pivot the boat until it's in a position where you can back row away from it long before reaching it. An angle of about 45 degrees is used cross-current and is known as ferrying. This both slows you down and allows lateral progress across the river. Remember that it's the back of the boat that needs to be pointed in the direction you want to go, not the front.

Most rowed boats respond rather slowly to the oars at first, so advance set-up is necessary. After pivoting or setting the boat up, begin an easy back stroke long before you reach your obstacle to get some momentum going. This usually takes several strokes to begin. As you more closely approach a hazard, you might need to back stroke harder. On the other hand, your first few back strokes may have built up enough momentum and carried you far enough to the side of it to suffice. Each encounter will be a little different.

You want to miss obstacles, but not by more than necessary when fishermen are aboard. Beginners have a tendency to over-row, taking ten ferrying back strokes to skirt an obstacle that only needs three strokes to miss. Instead of easing around a rock and missing it by 5 feet, they shoot across the river and miss it by 50. Over-rowing makes fishing much more difficult. Better safe than sorry, though, and yet over-rowing can get beginners in trouble in boulder-studded rapids, where the way in which you shave hazards and set up for the next one can be critical. Knowing how much power is needed to maneuver around objects in various situations takes experience. There are times and places when the elements will keep pushing you into the hazard you're trying to avoid, for instance, sharp swift bends in rivers, steep water-gathering drops, cross-winds, and side-slipping currents. Here, extra effort and quick decision making is in order. On a straight stretch of even-flowing river with no wind, pivoting and back-stroke ferrying can be quite leisurely.

The best thing to do is spend plenty of time at the oars under a good coach. Start out on forgiving rivers and progress to more difficult

Sharp bends in rivers can hide potential hazards from view. Rapids, logjams, and boulder gardens can suddenly materialize, calling for quick decision making and action. If you are ever in doubt, pull over to scout tricky spots.

ones as your proficiency develops. To be painfully literal, don't get in over your head right from the start. There are several drownings every year on Montana rivers. Most occur in spring and early summer, when rivers are high with snowmelt and ice cold. Floaters are eager to get on stream, especially the novices with new boats. New logjams may have formed since winter, and high water tends to shove boats right into obstacles at this time. Waves, holes, whirlpools, and turbulence are all bigger and faster during runoff. Unfortunately, many floaters look at a boat trip like it's some carnival ride—until they flip in frigid, roiling water, losing gear and risking life. The sudden uncontrollable shock of landing in freezing water and the resulting hypothermia quickly erode responsiveness and alert thought. Panic and senseless floundering often ensue. Many river drownings involve alcohol, and the absence of life jackets, let alone wet suits.

It's a good idea to row some white-water rivers as you progress in experience, to hone your rowing and water-reading skills and to build your knowledge and confidence. Decision making should become quick and comprehensive. Making rowing skills second nature is your goal. Other people's lives and property can be in your hands. Perhaps the biggest factors in proficient rowing are in your advance route planning and set-up, and in making back rowing a habit.

Basic Maneuvering

As I keep emphasizing, all of your maneuvering should be done with back strokes. The next habit to develop is that of pointing the stern (rear) of the boat in the direction you want to go. This is achieved through oar manipulation. We'll call it "pivoting." After the boat is pivoted, with the stern pointed in the direction you want to go, pull back on both oars, propelling the craft back and at a 45-degree angle to the current. Let's step back a bit and go through these maneuvers one at a time and look at each more closely.

PUTTING IN AND PUSHING OFF

The first thing you'll need to do is to launch your boat. Most put-ins are easy enough to negotiate, but in difficult pieces of water, even pushing off from the bank to start your float can be tricky. The current might want to immediately push you into a logjam or rock garden. The beginner will be hard-pressed to get it together in such situations.

The trick here is to get your boat's stern pointed in the right direction from the very start: upstream and at a 30–45-degree angle to the current. This is best achieved by having the boat "parallel parked" along the bank for starters. We'll presume there is a rower and two fishermen. The boat is held in place, but floating (not half hung-up on the bank), by the angling team. The rower can get in first so as to be instantly ready to row when the moment of truth comes.

The next steps in critical situations will require good timing, because a strong current can easily spin the boat out of control. The stern angler now pushes his end out to about a 30–45-degree angle across the current. This should put the boat at a good angle to ferry out to midstream and clear the oar from the bank so the rower will be able to get an immediate dig in the water. The stern angler quickly jumps in the boat, gets a good grip on something, and sits down.

Just moments after the stern fisher pushes off, the bow angler pushes the front of the boat straight back and jumps in. The idea is to push it straight back while it's still at the 30–45-degree ferrying angle to the current. If he waits too long to push off, the stern of the boat will be swung downstream by the force of the current. And if an immediate maneuver was needed to pull away from a hazard, the rower will be in a bad position to deal with it. It will take extra time and distance to spin the boat back to a good ferrying angle, especially if it's been spun all the way around and is now facing downstream rather than up. The bankside oar can also be inhibited by shallow water or the bank itself, because the current will most likely push the boat back toward shore.

Most put-ins or launch sites won't present a problem, but there certainly are instances where immediate control needs to be executed, and a novice won't have much if any time to figure much out about the rowing game. One common situation calling for immediate launch control is when floaters stop to scout a rapid, logjam, or other hazard before floating by it (always a good idea!). There can be just one good entry slot or chute leading into a rapid. The boat not only needs to be in that spot but might also need to be set up properly as it goes down the chute in order to begin the next boulder-dodging maneuver. Rapids wait for no one!

There are still other situations where the boat not only needs to be in the right spot, with the stern pointed the right way, but also needs to have some inertia built up through back rowing if it's going to miss the next quickly approaching hazard. Entry position, set-up or ferrying angle, and preestablished momentum can all be absolutely necessary in tight rowing situations. Consequently, after scouting a rapid, the need for a good push-off and launch facilitating immediate control can be critical. In serious situations, such entries need to be discussed so that everybody clearly understands what to do and when to do it.

The boat type has some bearing here. Rafts and prams have lower bows (front ends) and are generally easier to jump into after pushing off. Drift boats have high front ends and can be difficult to scale, especially for older and less athletic fishermen. In this case it's best for the bow and stern anglers to get in first, then the rower should push the boat out at the proper angle and quickly jump in. Most drift boats have anchor systems, too, which allow everyone to

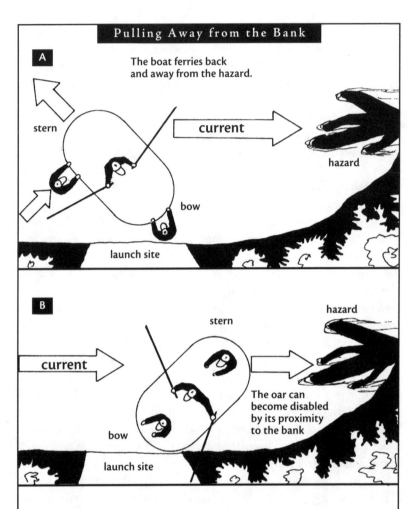

A. To pull away from the bank in complete control, the stern angler pushes the stern out to a near-45-degree ferrying angle and jumps in. The bow angler then pushes the boat straight back and gets in. The rower now pulls hard on both oars. He may need extra power on the midstream oar to keep the stern from being swung downstream.

B. A bad push-off can result in the stern being swung downstream by a strong current. The rower can get into a difficult position and have a hard time pulling away from the impending hazard.

get in the boat and get seated before the boatman angles the craft out across the currents.

When the oarsman is pushing out without an anchor system, he will also have to deal with the oars. These are usually in the locks and either trailing downstream in the water or pulled across and resting upon the gunwales (upper sides of the boat). In either case, he'll have to jump over or climb around the oars while getting to his seat. This too requires at least a little thought in critical situations.

A last hazard to avoid when launching is other people's boats. There are some beautiful new wooden and shiny fiberglass boats on the river these days. Their owners can get hot when some unskilled or mindless floater slams into the side of their craft, putting a big scar in it. A ding in some types of fine craft could cost hundreds of dollars to repair. Although some unthinking float fisherman might try to wave off denting someone else's boat, its owner, who might have spent hundreds of hours building and maintaining it, will be quite ready to shoot him! If you're a novice and have the choice, try launching downstream of other boats so you have open water to get established in.

PIVOTING

A boat is pivoted in one of two ways. You can leave one oar in place in the water, which acts as a brake on that side, and then take several backstrokes with the other oar. This will swing the stern around at an easy pace until it's pointed in the direction you want to go. It usually takes just a few oar strokes to pivot or turn a boat unless it's particularly heavy or you're in very turbulent water.

The second way to pivot is by pulling back with one oar and pushing forward with the other oar, rather than planting it as a brake. This speeds up the pivoting process, which can be important in some serious rock- or log-choked stretches of river where quick decision making and instant action are called for.

From a fishing point of view, a quick and sudden pivot is undesirable. A standing angler can be knocked over by vigorous pivoting, especially if it's unannounced. Indeed, when I row anglers, I often tell them in advance when I'm going to pivot or pull back extra hard on the oars, because either can cause standing anglers to fall down, even if they are in knee braces. What you want when rowing anglers is a

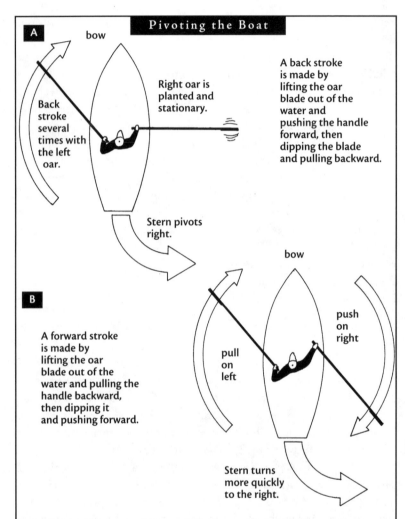

Pivoting the Boat

A

bow

Back stroke several times with the left oar.

Right oar is planted and stationary.

A back stroke is made by lifting the oar blade out of the water and pushing the handle forward, then dipping the blade and pulling backward.

Stern pivots right.

B

bow

A forward stroke is made by lifting the oar blade out of the water and pulling the handle backward, then dipping it and pushing forward.

pull on left

push on right

Stern turns more quickly to the right.

A. There are two common ways of pivoting, or turning. The first method uses only one oar for power. The right one in this case is "planted" as a brake that holds that side still while the left side pivots.

B. The second and faster method of turning is the push-pull pivot turn. In this case the left oar is pulled through the water and the right oar is pushed. This speedier way of pivoting takes a little practice to master and tends to confuse rowers at first.

very smooth and polished rowing cadence so as not to disrupt the fishing. Ideally, passengers should hardly feel your rowing strokes at all as you keep them in the ideal position in relation to their target water. Heavy water and river hazards can require vigorous rowing, though, and passengers should be alerted to your course of action so they can secure themselves. It's not that rare for a rower to actually dump a stern angler right into the river on an abrupt pivot or stronger-than-average oar stroke! Communication is the key here.

The push-pull pivot takes practice to become instinctual. Most beginners have a little trouble remembering which oar to do what with for a while. The best thing to do is get out on a mellow river and pivot, ferry, and pivot again like crazy. Do it dozens of times, until it starts coming naturally. You don't want to draw a mental blank when you suddenly find yourself in a tricky spot!

FERRYING

This is a common term for crossing a river or its currents (currents don't always run parallel to the river's banks). By rowing at roughly a 45-degree angle with your stern leading the way, you can cross a river without being swept too far downstream. In mellow flows you can actually row upstream against the current and cross to the other side.

By having your boat at a 45-degree angle, the current coming downstream will deflect off the craft's side, helping to push it in the intended direction. In contrast, rowing a boat completely sideways to the current will be a noticeable change. The full force of the current will grab the craft and push it downstream, perhaps farther than you want to go.

There can be serious consequences when pulling out and crossing a river directly sideways to the current. Power currents and waves can easily flip boats that don't enter them at the ferrying angle. In fact, you might want to enter a very strong current at less than a 45-degree angle and more of a 30-degree one. It's the moment you first enter a rushing current that presents the problem. This generally occurs when you pull away from the bank during a launch or when you pull out of midriver eddies (such as from downstream of boulders, bridge pilings, or islands). A sideways entry puts the almost stationary boat

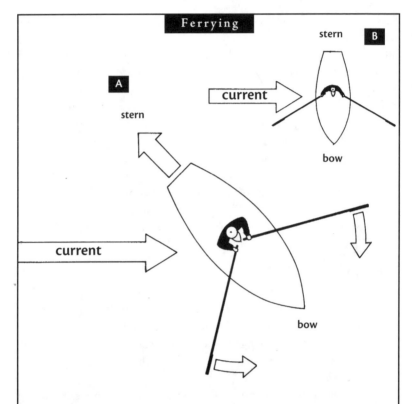

A. The boatman back rows at about a 45-degree angle to the current to cross a river. The current deflects off the upstream side of the boat, helping to push it in the right direction. This allows the boat to cross without being swept too far downstream. Note that river currents don't always flow parallel to the banks.

B. If a boat is angled too straight across the river, it will suddenly be shoved downstream at a more rapid rate, at actual current speed. This could mean zipping by some valuable fishing water on the other side!

immediately out into a rushing torrent in extreme cases. The water will pile up against the upstream side of the boat and tend to climb up over the gunwale and shove it under. The end result can be an alarmingly fast and disconcerting flip. It happens quite frequently to beginners on powerful rivers, most often when they are high with snowmelt and deadly cold. Low-sided craft, including canoes, prams, and small rafts, flip easiest, but even big rafts and drift boats go over every year. When a boat enters a strong current at a 15–45-degree back-ferrying angle, the water pushes against or slides under the stern, which is much less likely to flip it. This is why modern rafts, drift boats, and prams have upturned bows and sterns (called "rocker") to allow the current to slide under the boat and push it up rather than under. Flat-bottomed boats and canoes (those without any rocker) are much more likely to be rolled and flipped under similar conditions and are harder to navigate where constant maneuvering is required, even when rowed by very competent hands.

Think about what water will do to your craft and where it will be carried before entering strong or dangerous flows. Be prepared to row strongly, make fast decisions, and do some quick powerhouse pivot turns. In these more extreme cases passengers should be seated, wearing life jackets, and holding on! They might even want to have an extra paddle or oar on hand to help with any last-second maneuvering. Again, we're talking about extreme cases here, but those are just the ones you want to understand and train yourself for. Rivers can be unforgiving!

Once you're safely out in the current, ferrying over to wherever it is you want to go, things should go a little easier because you're now traveling closer to, but slower than, river speed. Some basic maneuvering will soon come in to play. Rocks, logs, bridge abutments, gravel bars, and the like will need to be assessed and rowed around. At the same time, you'll be slowing the craft down, putting anglers in the best position to realize the fishing potential.

You will find that it takes several oar strokes before a boat starts building up much ferrying momentum. This is why preplanning your pivot turns and ferrying maneuvers is necessary. Last-second decisions don't always get carried off very well! The boat will also continue the side-ferrying momentum for a while after you actually stop rowing. With practice, you'll get used to these momentum factors; they're important to the proper navigation of the boat.

Another concern in ferrying is the depth of the river. You want to be continually shifting your field of vision to include all your rowing contingencies. This not only includes figuring your rowing route and

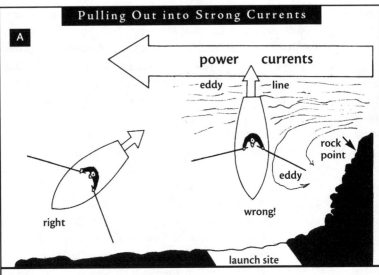

Pulling Out into Strong Currents

A

power　currents

eddy — line

rock point

eddy

wrong!

right

launch site

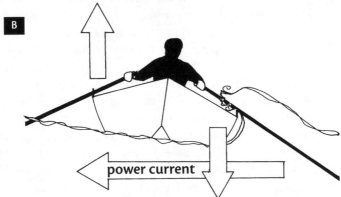

B

power current

A. When pulling out into a strong current, drop downstream a bit from eddy zones of great current-speed contrast. Keep a sharp 30-degree or so ferrying angle to the current when first entering it so that the swift water slides under your stern.

B. If you pull out into a powerful current from an eddy with your boat sideways to the current, water will tend to heave up and possibly over the upstream side. In extreme cases this can shove the upstream side of your boat under the water, rolling and flipping it. This is a frequent occurrence with novice rowers, especially in low-sided craft.

how far you are from the angler's target water, but you also need to be alert to the depth of the water in which you're about to stick your oar. You might remember our earlier discussion about not digging the oar blade very deeply in the water. This is especially important when you're somewhat or completely sideways to the current, for then your downstream oar could potentially jam blade-first into the streambed. Boulders or logs could be jutting up toward the surface, or the river could be shallow near the banks. In any case, you need to be aware of river depth and to pay particular attention to the downstream oar's field of play. Jamming the downstream oar into the bottom during a ferry will wake you right up. The oar blade can be broken, or it can wedge between rocks. In heavier currents, the boat might wheel out of control while you reset the oar, which has likely been blown from its oar lock. Boats can even be flipped if low-sided craft get a downstream oar jammed in a swift current, for the boat is brought to a sudden stop and water begins climbing the upstream side. A downstream oar can also be knocked loose from the rower's grip if it jams into the streambed. Lost oars are common occurrences in these situations, unless you have the foresight to either tie the oars in beforehand or to use oar stirrups.

Another type of ferrying incident happens often enough on big western rivers, where the wind can really whip. A downstream gale will start blowing drift boats downstream at a much faster rate than the current if the oarsman lets it get out of control. And because drift boats have a lot of rocker, or an upturned hull fore and aft, they blow like leaves and consequently are pushed into a sideways position to the current. When the rower of a side-blown drift boat dips his downstream oar in the river (especially after *not* rowing for a while and letting the boat's downstream speed greatly exceed the current speed), that downstream oar can act like a sudden brake. This problem is usually limited to boats with horn oar locks, where the rower's grip must maintain the oar-blade angle. For if the blade gets turned sideways a little, the boat's windblown momentum shoves the oar down deeper, where its steep angle brakes the boat to a sudden stop. The boat will lurch over, being partly pulled under on the downstream side by the oar's diving impetus, and partly pushed up on the upstream side by the wind. The sudden jolt of the oar's braking action can even throw everybody out of their seats and to the downstream

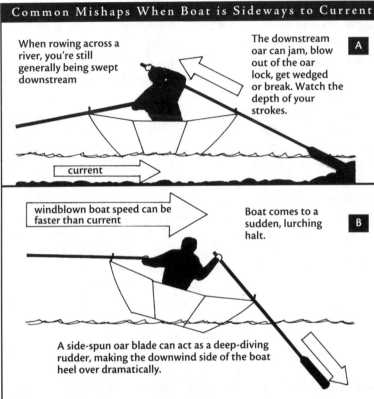

Common Mishaps When Boat is Sideways to Current

When rowing across a river, you're still generally being swept downstream

The downstream oar can jam, blow out of the oar lock, get wedged or break. Watch the depth of your strokes.

A

current

windblown boat speed can be faster than current

Boat comes to a sudden, lurching halt.

B

A side-spun oar blade can act as a deep-diving rudder, making the downwind side of the boat heel over dramatically.

A. When rowing across shallow reaches of a river, watch the bottom for depth and how deeply you dig your downstream oar. It's common to jam the downstream oar blade into the river bottom, which can give the boat a serious jolt and sudden canter. It can also break or wedge oar blades on the bottom and pop oars from their locks. This has the potential to ruin your set-up when entering a challenging bit of water. Another common occurrence is when an oar hits the river bottom, blows out of the lock, and jams the oar handle into your side or face! This has happened to me more than once and can really hurt.

B. When a downriver wind is howling, your boat can be going faster than the current. If you stop rowing, the boat will blow sideways. Beginning rowers tend to get fatigued and take a rest, then start back up as they approach a hazard. Should the downstream oar blade be planted horizontally rather than vertically, it will dig deep, causing its side of the boat to suddenly halt, dive, and lurch. I've been in situations where this almost flipped the boat!

side. This makes that side, which is already diving a bit, go down even farther. Flips in such cases are not out of the question. I was in a couple of these incidents a couple years back on the wide Missouri, with a novice at the oars. It wasn't that he was a complete novice, just a novice at rowing in 40–60 mph winds, something a guide has to face every few days! When in high-wind situations, row in total control or get off the river for a while.

Most of your ferrying experiences will be of the easy and enjoyable sort, an exuberant oneness with your boat. Do, however, take note of how these factors affect your rowing. Become aware of your and your boat's limitations in more intense encounters.

THE BASIC MANEUVER AROUND A RIVER HAZARD

The diagram on page 32 and steps below describe a basic sequence of maneuvers for negotiating a path around a river hazard. Further complexities can arise when crosscurrents, side winds, heavy water and turbulence, or multiple rock maneuvers become involved. Though these factors add challenges that call for more thought, the basic rowing maneuvers remain the same.

Step 1

The first step in navigating an obstacle is to *clearly recognize its presence* early on and *plan your upcoming route* and the maneuvering needed to follow it. This should be formulating as soon as the hazard comes into view, not when the boat is pressed up face-to-face with it!

Step 2

Having recognized the danger and figured out the preferred route around it (to the midriver side in the illustration), the boat is pivot-turned or set up by pulling back on the left oar several times while planting the right oar or pushing forward on it once or twice. The boat is now angled properly to begin a back-rowing ferry out of the rock's path and toward midriver, about 45 degrees.

Step 3

Several back strokes with both oars now build up enough momentum to ferry the boat out of the rock's path. In many cases this

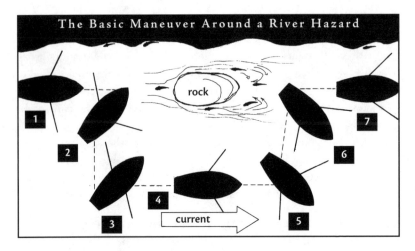

The Basic Maneuver Around a River Hazard

will only require three to six oar strokes. In a twisting river with powerful currents it might take several more. At the same time, you're still trying to slow the boat down and put anglers in a good position to fish around the boulder, the bank, or both. There are times, of course, when safety will outride fishing considerations and the boat may have to be rowed away from the best theoretic fishing position. On the other hand, beginning rowers do have a tendency to row farther away from an obstacle than necessary, making fishing more difficult. Only experience will teach you how many oar strokes will be needed to move the boat such and such a distance in such and such a current. It can take as few as two to four back strokes to move the boat far enough after the pivot has been achieved. In any case, remember that the stern (rear) of the boat should always be pointed away from the obstacle and toward the best escape route as you approach it. Pointing the stern straight upcurrent is not the correct ferrying angle!

STEP 4

After ferrying to the midriver side of the rock (smoothly, so as not to jostle passengers more than necessary) and lining up in a good fishing drift lane to go by it, the boat is straightened in the current by a few pulls on the right oar while you plant and drag the left. This will straighten you back up. Now continue an easy back-rowing pace to slow the craft down as you float-fish your way on by it. Fish are likely to be found upstream, tucked right along the sides, and in the eddy line and downstream eddy of midriver boulders. Don't neglect running a fly by all these locations in succession. In a slow- to medium-flowing river, the oarsman can back row the boat to a standstill, allowing a few extra drifts of the flies. Anglers should be consciously targeting different spots for maximum teamwork efficiency. This can be agreed to prior to the approach, thus keeping the two anglers from jamming out their casts to the same spot at the same time, which some trout find unnerving!

Step 5

Having gone by the rock and now intending to get back to the fish-sheltering banks, pivot the boat again, with the stern pointed at a 45-degree angle toward shore. This is done by pulling on the right oar several times while planting or pushing forward on the left oar.

Step 6

Once you have angled the boat properly, a few pulls on both oars should get you back in casting range of the bank. Eddies behind rocks help suck the boat in behind them, too, which can reduce the number of oar strokes needed to realign with the bank. On whitewater stretches these eddies are used in various ways to enhance navigation. They can be used to slow the boat down or even come to a standstill, allowing a little rest while you scrutinize the rowing path yet to come.

When water is pouring over boulders, these more turbulent eddies become known as "holes." We'll discuss these in Chapter 3, for they can be quite dangerous and easily flip boats. Don't cut in too closely behind large-volume flows over big boulders. Their tendency is to suck a boat quickly in right behind them, spin it sideways, fill it with water, and perhaps flip it.

Step 7

Once the boat has been ferried back to the desired distance from shore, drag the right oar and pull back a few times on the left. This straightens the boat out again for further fishing progress along the banks. Keep a steady but not too taxing back-rowing pace to improve the fishing possibilities.

On rock-studded rivers maneuvering will be constant, varied, and fun. Once it becomes second nature you'll find you can row, look for rising fish, duck bad casts, and sip on a drink simultaneously, all while analyzing the best rowing route and most likely fish-holding water!

Once rowing skills become habitual and second nature, you'll be able to concentrate more on the fishing possibilities. This will take time spent on the river, but when you find you don't have to think about the rowing much anymore, you'll be well on your way. It's then that you'll start noticing more subtle rising fish, trouty seams you may never have noticed before, and the shape of fish under clear water. You can now be the trout hunter, with little to distract you from that focus.

Before going on to a discussion of river hazards and fishing skills though, I want to introduce you to a rowing method that's largely unknown to most floaters. Fishing guides who have discovered it use it extensively. It allows the best fine-tuned positioning, keeping anglers in the best casting positions more of the time. We call it the crawl stroke. It's the focus of Chapter 2.

2

THE CRAWL STROKE

*Y*ears of rowing on smaller rivers with lots of rocks to dodge inspired me and other guides to perfect some variant rowing skills. These differ from white-water skills somewhat, because the force of the water, turbulence, and waves are rarely part of our float-fishing game. It's a subtlety of oar strokes that counts in fishing, rowing to keep anglers in the best possible position while slowing the craft to a standstill—all done so smoothly that passengers hardly know you're rowing. The boat and anglers aren't jerked around by unnecessary or violent pivots. One strategy, for example, is to go over shallow rocks with a raft, high-centering them rather than rowing around them. The raft floor stretches up and over rounded shallow or even protruding rocks quite easily. At low water it's a nonstop rock-dodging game. High-centering some rocks allows you to keep a straighter rowing track down the river, avoiding pivot maneuvers whenever possible. This is to improve the anglers' position in the river in relation to their target water. In very shallow areas and when going over shallow tailout gravel bars, such rocks can also indicate the deepest water path, because the streambed around them tends to erode more deeply than the rest of the streambed. This is just one example of more tactical rowing strategies for low-water fishing.

Unnecessary pivoting and ferrying makes fishing decidedly more difficult and annoying. Fly-line length has to be rapidly and constantly

Shallow summer rivers can call for special rowing adaptations such as the crawl stroke.

changed. Just as an angler is about to drop a fly on some hot spot, an over-rowed boat can yank it away. It's the smoothest, straightest course you should row, one that allows anglers to use a steady length of fly line. You shouldn't be too near the target water, which scares fish, or so far as to make presentations difficult. There is usually an ideal distance to be maintained, and it does take a degree of constant awareness to maintain it. There's nothing more annoying than trying to fish from a poorly rowed boat.

The rowing technique I'm about to describe came naturally to me, but only after years of low-water rowing experience. Even today, more than ten years later, it's rare for me to see anyone else on the river using this rowing style.

The crawl stroke is a combination of two distinctly different rowing techniques: back rowing and sweeping. Sweeping is an old and localized method of rowing where the oars are stationed at the front and rear of the boat, rather than at the sides. Such oars are big, long, and often rowed by one rower per oar, who stands up. Sweeps were commonly used in the 1800s on various types of rafts (including bundled logs being navigated downstream to mills) and on flatboats such as those that took immigrants down the Ohio River in the days of early westward expansion. Some of these rafts and flatboats were quite large. The only rivers I'm aware of where sweep oars are seen today are some Idaho rivers, where a few tour operators still use them on large rafts.

Naturally, a boat with oars on the front and back can only be rowed sideways. Such craft "go with the flow" when out in the currents but are swept sideways with the oars to slower inside bends and eddies to land and to dodge hazards. Big rafts and sweep boats used by the pioneers might have oars on the sides as well as the ends, plus poles to push with off the bottom, and perhaps even a sail. Pioneer and fur-trading history makes for some very interesting reading, for these boaters not only drifted down into uncertain waters and futures, but they also had to contend with storms, floods, ice, Native Americans whose lands they were trespassing on, and even organized bands of river pirates.

The crawl stroke crosses back rowing with sweeping. The end result is that you can row the boat sideways while keeping it parallel to the banks! This rowing technique has never been fully appreciated by the vast majority of recreational rowers, or guides, for that matter. The benefit is that you can eliminate a high percentage of standard pivot turns, making it easier for anglers, and especially the stern angler, to fish. It's the stern angler who's affected most by maneuvering, because the stern is the end being pivoted and redirected the most. The stern angler also has to cast over the oars, something we'll look at later. The boatman is usually rowing to position the bow angler in the best location, with the stern angler working with whatever boat angle is handed him. This is why the crawl stroke is so good for fishing. Both anglers can be kept in the best possible position more of the time. The crawl is also a smooth oar stroke. Because the boat is nothing more than a platform for anglers to cast off of, the steadier and smoother one can row it, the better its fishing potential.

Here's how the crawl stroke works. As you back row with one hand (the left one in the illustration), you sweep with the right one.

Sweeping pushes water sideways under the boat rather than parallel to its course. This is achieved by pointing the right oar forward rather than to the side (this calls for a change in hand position), dipping it in the water a few feet to the bow side of the boat, then pushing on it.

This feels unnatural at first. You'll likely have trouble initially grasping the concept. It's a lot like the old rub your belly while patting your head routine. It does take practice to make it come naturally.

There are a couple of prerequisites to doing the crawl. First, the boat needs to be cocked slightly, with the stern angled in the direction you're crawling (which is the direction you want to go) about 15 degrees. This calls for a very minor pivot before the first crawl stroke can be made, and one that doesn't interrupt the fishing.

The second element that's necessary is an oar lock that's positioned at the widest point of the boat's gunwale, but it's even better if it actually protrudes out beyond the boat's sides. This configuration is most commonly found on rafts where the metal rowing frame and oar-lock stands stick out sideways beyond the raft's tubes. The farther beyond the side of the boat the oar lock is fabricated (within reason), the more effective the crawl, because the oarsman can then push water farther sideways under the bow of the boat.

An oarsman doing the crawl stroke looks a little ungainly at first sight. He leans sideways rhythmically with each oar stroke, twisting his body somewhat, rather than leaning back. This is due to the pushing out on the crawling or sweeping oar that pushes the water sideways under the boat. He pulls on one oar while pushing sideways with the other.

There's no doubt that this rowing style is harder on wrists and elbows. After more than twenty years of rowing, my wrists and elbows are starting to give me some problems. This is not a rowing style that's powerful enough for heavy-water maneuvering or strong crosswinds, either. What it is ideal for is fishing, for subtle maneuvering around rocks while largely eliminating those strong pivot turns that give the stern angler casting problems. I'd say I use the crawl stroke at least 50 percent of the rowing day and perhaps 75 percent of the time on low-water, rock-dodging rivers. It's that effective.

The crawl stroke has a couple of other practical uses, too. The first one comes in handy for "grabbing eddies." When I pass a boulder

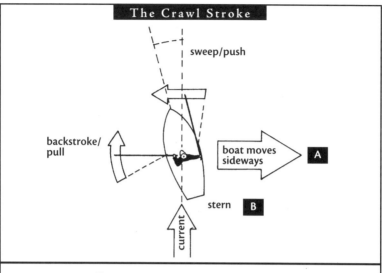

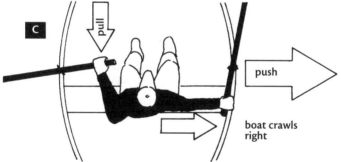

A. The crawl stroke allows a boat to be rowed sideways while still being slowed for fishing. One oar is pulled as usual, the other is pointed downstream and is pushed.

B. The stern is cocked to about a 15-degree angle to the current and points slightly in the direction the boat will travel.

C. The crawl stroke calls for a change in hand positioning as the right oar in the illustration is swung into a sweeping position. The oar is then dipped and pushed rather than pulled. The sweep stroke is a short one, but enough to move the boat sideways toward the sweep-oar side.

or island and wish to pull in behind it, my downstream-pointed sweep oar is grabbed by the back-swirling eddy water, which helps pull the boat in.

Another case involves the eddies found on the inside bends of rivers, which are also good places to find a fish or two. (I use this application most on small rivers, when I don't want to get swept out to the outside bend or undercut bank side, which the current naturally tends to do.) After the anglers pop a couple of quick casts ahead of the boat and into the eddy line and eddy, the boatman can use this eddy line in helping to navigate a sharp bend in the river. There also tend to be fish along the outside of the bend, where deeper, swifter water is generally found, with some good big fish-holding pockets. As the rower approaches the river's bend and perceives the need to start powering away from the fast water outside of the bend, he can do a slight pivot as needed, then begin crawling over toward the inside bend. Anglers will want to give their attention to the inside bend before the boat floats through it with some almost straight downstream casts. By crawling over to the inside-point eddy line, the boat will be in a good position to slow down while switching the fishing focus to the outside bank. The sweeping oar, which is pointing downstream on the inside-bend side, will be grabbed somewhat by the eddying water there. This actually helps draw the boat into the eddy, turning it naturally, and often matches the curve of the bend in the river. The boat turns on its own with the sweep oar producing a ruddering effect as its caught in the inside-bend eddy. This is more clear on the river, once you've played with it, than it sounds on paper. I use this dodge frequently.

When rowing on more powerful white-water rivers, the crawl stroke isn't always strong enough. Quickly revert back to the pivot and back-row style in this situation.

One thing you do have to watch for and be aware of when crawling is the depth of the water and presence of rocks. This is especially true when crawling over to shallower inside bends. Because the oar is pointed straight downstream, it can and does jam into the bottom on occasion, with the weight of the boat bearing down on it. Because most oar locks allow the oar to come free in this situation, one must keep a grip on the oar so it doesn't fall overboard. Most oar-lock

Using the Crawl Stroke with Eddies

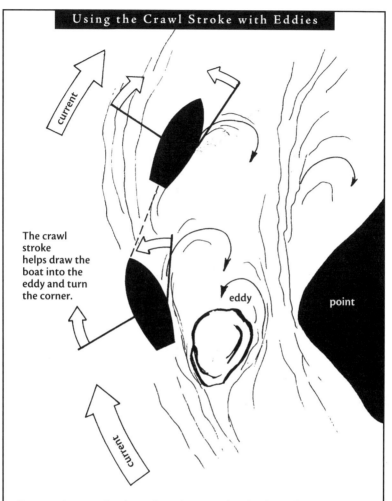

current

The crawl
stroke
helps draw the
boat into the
eddy and turn
the corner.

eddy

point

current

Because a boat coming down the main current is going faster than the currents
in an eddy (some of which are actually going back upstream), the sweeping oar
has a pronounced front-ruddering effect. The boat tends to go in the direction
in which the submerged sweep oar is pointing. (To the right, in the illustration.
Continued back strokes with the left oar will be needed to keep the boat from
spinning in a circle.) You'll feel a heavy pull on the sweep oar as it grabs those
currents and gets sucked into the eddy. In very powerful rivers this will be too
hard on your arm, so quickly revert to normal pivoting and back rowing. Otherwise, the crawl stroke helps steer you into eddies and around corners with a
minimum of pivot turns.

systems do have a retentive feature to keep the oars from coming off too easily. What can happen, though, is the fracturing and breaking of oar blades. I've also had oar blades jam straight in between rocks so tightly that I could hardly get them back out, especially once the boat starts spinning out of control in the currents, levering the oar blade in even tighter. I've snapped a few blades in this fashion over the years. I'm sure this presents a rather comic scene to bystanders, me standing and yanking on the oar and yelling at it while spinning in circles and stuck midstream. In any case, remain aware of river depth and bottom structure when crawling in the shallows.

One last application of the crawl stroke is for hugging the banks in very narrow channels where going down the middle would eliminate most of the fishing possibilities. This usually occurs when a small river is broken up into several channels by islands. Rowing the usual way calls for enough water to the sides of the boat for full oar extension, as well as enough depth to gain a scoop of water. Get too close and the oar hits the bottom or the bank itself.

The crawl stroke allows you to move in closer to a bank with the sweeping oar parallel to the bank side. It works more as a rudder here, with only short little corrective strokes being possible, but they are usually enough. Here again, the water eddies, this time off the edges of the bank, tend to keep the boat and sweep oar sucked in to it. The outer oar can be pushed, pulled, or just planted to maintain some forward progress while keeping the craft parallel to the shore.

Another use of the sweeping oar comes in here, that of pushing the water away from the boat while crawling, instead of underneath it. This reverse crawl is usually necessary part of the time when slinking along close to a bank, because the river's current tends to push the boat, and especially the front of the boat, into the bank. We're generally dealing with mild edge-water currents in such cases, and this application of the crawl and reverse crawl works well in these situations. Just be sure to watch how deeply you dig your sweeping blade, because you're hovering in the shallows. Each dig of the crawling oar should be shallow and quick, perhaps burying only half the blade in the water.

This bank-hugging technique is used most when there are miles yet to be floated, for otherwise, time allowing, it would be better to

Hugging a Bank with the Crawl Stroke

current

island

Watch for tall
grasses and
trees on your
backcast!

The crawl stroke allows you to hug a bank more closely than you can rowing conventionally. I find this most useful when floating through small side channels that I don't have the time or desire to stop and wade-fish. In this way I can still fish the middle and far bank without floating down the middle and scaring all the fish in the channel. The sweep oar can push water either way for fine maneuvering. It often scrapes the bottom, as might the boat, being in such close proximity to the bank.

pull over, anchor, and wade-fish small side channels. If you need to keep some forward progress going, though, hugging the banks allows anglers to continue fishing the middle and far side of a small channel. Their casts will need to be more downstream and ahead of the boat than normal, though, so that the trout see the fly before they see the boat. Watch out for tall streamside foliage behind you! It's best to look back before each backcast when hugging the banks.

STANDARD CRAWL-STROKE MANEUVER
STEP 1

As always, rowing course and hazards are observed and assessed as early as possible (see illustration on page 45).

STEP 2

A very easy pivot is made by dragging the right oar for a second while continuing to back row once or twice with the left. You're only looking to achieve about a 15–20-degree angle against the current here, which isn't enough to really interfere with the stern angler's casting. As soon as the boat achieves this slight angle, the right oar is lifted from the water and swung till the blade is pointing downstream. This calls for a switch of the arm and hand position on the oar, and a posture that's somewhat like leaning against the handrail of a staircase or escalator.

STEP 3

This is the tricky part for beginners. Continue back rowing with the left oar while you sweep with the right. The 15–20-degree cant of the boat to the current is maintained throughout. The sweep stroke is made by dipping the oar blade in the water a few feet out from the boat's bow side, then pushing the oar handle outward with your arm until the blade almost hits the front side of the boat. It's then quickly lifted from the water and swept back out for the next oar stroke. This pushes water mostly sideways under the craft, with the oar also acting somewhat as a front-end rudder, or steering device. The stroke with the sweep-oar arm is usually enhanced with a little sideways "body English," with the rower leaning into the oar for greater leverage, because this is a relatively weak arm position.

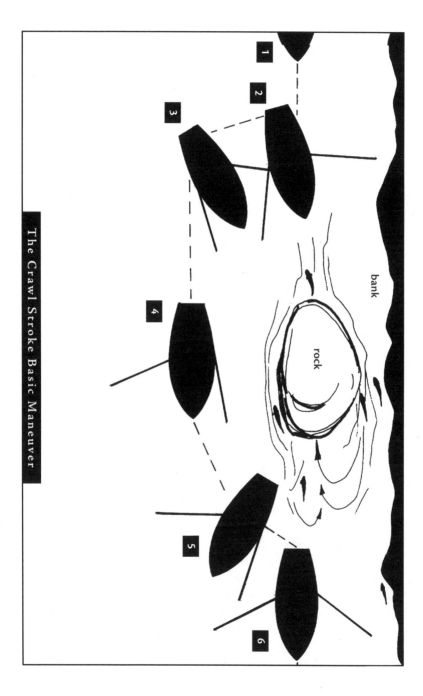

The Crawl Stroke Basic Maneuver

STEP 4

Once you've crawled or side-rowed your boat out far enough to miss and fish the boulder, straighten up by dragging your left oar, switching your right hand grip back to a normal rowing position, and making one or two right-hand back strokes.

If it seems as though the crawl stroke isn't moving you sideways fast enough to miss the boulder, immediately pivot the stern farther out to the 45-degree ferrying angle with your left oar, reset the right oar to a normal back-rowing position, and heave on both oars to get out of the area. Quick decisions and good early judgment are always advised. With practice, though, you'll find you can crawl to the side of most river obstacles in mellower flows.

STEP 5

After fishing in front, along the sides, and behind the boulder, angle the stern 15–20 degrees back toward the shore by dragging your left oar and pulling a couple times on the right. Reposition the left-hand oar grip to the sweeping position and crawl your way back to bank-fishing range.

STEP 6

Drag the right oar, reposition the left hand to the normal back-rowing position, and pull a couple times on the left oar to straighten and float-fish your way down the bank. The crawl is especially beneficial for maintaining the same distance from the bank, even when there are no obstacles to row around.

At first glance it might seem that all this hand and oar position changing might be more work than it's worth. For me, that's not the case. When I am rowing, there is plenty of added hand and oar maneuvering going on, sometimes every five to ten seconds. It looks a little more frantic to an observer (such as the angler in the stern of my boat). The end result, however, and the one I as a guide am considering most, is that it greatly modifies the effects of pivot turns, keeping a smoother, steadier course. This allows better fishing opportunities for both bow and stern anglers.

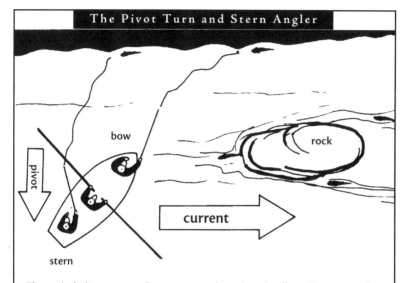

The typical pivot turn used to row around an obstacle affects the stern angler in two ways. First, it swings his end of the boat farther away from the target water, dragging his fly from it. Second, his line and the oar (the left one in the illustration) now cross paths. Tangles between the two are common. The stern angler must lift his rod and line to allow the oar to pass underneath it. This is another reason why the crawl stroke can be advantageous in rowing anglers.

Another plus from the stern angler's point of view is that when a rower is crawling, he doesn't have to contend with the oar. In normal back-rowing situations, the stern angler has to cast over the oar a good percentage of the time, holding his rod up a bit to allow the oar to pass underneath it. Tangles of oars and the stern angler's fly line are common otherwise. With the crawl stroke, the sweeping oar is pointed forward, usually on the side being fished, and it is out of the way of both anglers' fly lines. The stern angler does, however, have to be aware of changes in oar positioning as the rower switches styles to meet current demands.

I use the crawl stroke a lot for subtle distance compensations, even when no real obstacles are in the way. There are many other factors that affect a boat's position in relation to the banks, including cross-winds, crosscurrents, and bends in the river (which usually concentrate currents to the deeper, outside shore of the bend). To keep the perfect fly-casting distance away from a bank (or other target water), say 40–50 feet, requires constant attention to and adjustment for these factors. Most can be anticipated, preassessed, and set up for. When rowing anglers, more time is usually spent repositioning the boat to maintain an ideal casting position than in avoiding obstacles. This is where the crawl stroke is so valuable.

For instance, if the wind has blown you sideways a bit (a common occurrence in the West), you can make an almost imperceptible pivot, then crawl your way back to the proper distance from shore and straighten. Passengers hardly notice you're doing it. Compare this to the back-rowing method, where the boat is pivoted at a greater angle, back rowed a few strokes, and pivoted again. This affects the stern fisherman more, and jostles both anglers to a greater degree.

What I seem to do a high percentage of the time is to cock the boat slightly and position one oar or the other to sweep almost continuously. Crawl right a bit, then back left, perhaps back rowing with both oars for a little while, then back to a right crawl, and so it goes all day. I'm rowing for a paying angler's pleasure and perhaps putting out a more concentrated effort for a greater part of the day than the average recreational floater would. But once one is used to the crawl stroke, it will prove to be an ideal rowing technique for the fine-tuned positioning of a fishing boat, despite its ungainly appearance.

There is one more aspect of the crawl stroke that I find important in mid- to late summer when rivers are very low. Currents have slowed, rock evasion is frequently necessary, and the time it takes to get down a long reach of river has increased dramatically when compared to the high-water flows of spring and early summer. What the crawl stroke does at this time is to allow side-to-side maneuvering without slowing to the degree the normal back-row–pivot–back-row technique does. This may sound like a small point, but being able to gauge your speed and mileage over a particular stretch of time is an art. If you want to float a 15-mile stretch from 7 A.M. to 6 P.M., fish it hard, and not have to row out late in the dark or row through several miles of perfect water because you wasted too much time early on, you need to know how to gauge your progression over the course of the day. Getting to the take-out earlier than planned can be just as bad as getting in way too late, in the eyes of an angler. Arriving on time and maximizing the fishing potential within the allotted time takes plenty of experience.

In low-water rock-dodging extremes, the crawl stroke allows me to maneuver efficiently yet keep the boat moving forward enough to keep to my schedule. I go slow enough to fish well but don't bog down to a near standstill by using back-stroke maneuvering. On some of our backcountry multiday float trips we have some long-mileage, low-water days. The experienced guides will make it down to camp at just the right time for dinner. New and inexperienced boatmen will get to camp too early, too late, or even after dark. Of course, if a great hatch experience and super fishing slowed them down, it's okay!

How hard you back row varies with water level. The high-water season calls for a vigorous back-rowing pace so you don't blow through a day's fishing water in half a day. High water can also mean greatly reduced wade-fishing potential with more time and mileage spent fishing from the boat. Back rowing like mad early in the season is tough on your muscles and hands!

Low water presents the opposite problem—too much good-looking and wadable water with too many slow-flowing miles of river left to go. It's here that the easy-paced crawl stroke comes in so handy. It allows a steadier forward progress, when desired. If your chosen daily mileage can't be adjusted, your rowing pace and style must make up for it.

3

UNDERSTANDING MOVING WATER: RIVER HAZARDS AND HOW TO AVOID THEM

*M*any of the West's most productive trout rivers are easily navigated. Although hazards exist, they are easily handled by knowledgeable and observant rowers. Most of the actual oar time is spent slowing and positioning the boat to improve fishing. Nevertheless, an understanding of river hazards and the power of moving water is a must for all floaters.

The majority of river drownings are due to ignorance of river conditions, poor rowing or paddling skills, or insufficient or inadequate equipment. Rivers don't always give you the luxury of time to debate varied and sundry rowing options as they shove you toward a logjam. You need to understand the inherent qualities of moving water and its response to obstacles in its path. Water will shape streambeds in a predictable sequence of bends, riffles, and pools until it meets solid bedrock, tumbled boulders, and timber fall. Knowing how moving water responds to such impediments makes decision making quicker and navigation surer.

An experienced rower, for instance, will know that a sharp bend in a river will concentrate a stronger flow to the outside bend of the corner. He'll instinctively spin his stern toward the inside bend and start back rowing toward it before getting into the bend itself. A novice often lets the river almost shove him into the outside-bend bank before rowing like mad at the last second to pull away. It's a preassess-

Whoops—a classic wrap! The upstream side of this raft was shoved underwater after the raft collided with a boulder. Failing to recognize hazards, or indecision in maneuvering around them, often results in such accidents.

ment of what the water is likely to do that allows experienced boatmen to set up, that all-important element of more technical rowing.

The hazards we'll discuss are common on many rivers. Additional water volume (high water to flood stage) and current speed will increase navigational difficulties. Extreme low water makes it hard to get a bladefull of water at times, which also makes maneuvering difficult with oars. Bouncing off a low-water rock just before entering a tricky chute can throw you totally off course. In any case, treat all hazards with respect. Observe them coming, plan your route, and, with the techniques described in Chapters 1 and 2, set up your boat in advance. With the proper assessment and set-up, the avoidance maneuver itself often requires just a few well-timed oar strokes to skirt you around a hazard in safety.

Wrapping Boulders and Flipping in Holes

Having already discussed the basic rowing maneuver to ferry around a rock or boulder in Chapter 1, we'll now look at what happens if you actually hit one. We'll also take a close look at the hole water creates when it pours over barely submerged boulders and ledges.

What commonly happens when a raft (or drift boat) hits a boulder is: (1) a sudden impact occurs that can be more jolting than you might imagine. It can knock people out of their seats and toss gear overboard; (2) the boat might just bounce and spin off the rock, creating the possibility of dislodging, losing overboard, or even breaking an oar; (3) the boat can flip or wrap around the boulder.

When a boat slams into a boulder, it's usually because the boatman didn't set up and begin a back-rowing ferry away from it early enough in the game. (There are rock-choked channels where it's impossible not to hit a rock or two.) Most boulders will be hit by the boat at some sort of a sideways angle, with the rower making a last-ditch attempt to pull away from it. Occasionally a boat will plow nose-first into a boulder. This tends to happen with novices who are completely out of control, or in tight rock gardens when obstacles are coming at you so fast that any mistake is likely to get you in trouble. It's not unusual to be rowing down a rocky channel and "blow out" an oar by jamming it into a shallow rock. The time it takes to reposition an oar in the oar lock in such a case can be just long enough to totally foul up your route plan and set-up, resulting in a pinball escapade, where the boat bounces through the rest of the run. I occasionally hit rocks while watching my anglers' dry flies dancing along on the currents (I like to watch trout take them as much as the anglers do). The front ends of drift boats are high enough to block much of the forward view, especially when the bow angler is standing up and casting. In rock-dodging runs, extra attention must be paid to every detail of the channel.

Slamming into rocks can easily cause loose pieces of equipment on the deck of a drift boat or the sides of a raft to fly overboard. Many rods, cameras, and the like are lost and sunk every year. If you know you're about to enter a challenging bit of water, all gear should be tied down and secured, and life jackets donned. Though most fly fishermen don't like to wear life jackets because they interfere with casting and comfort, one should at least have the common sense to know when to put them on.

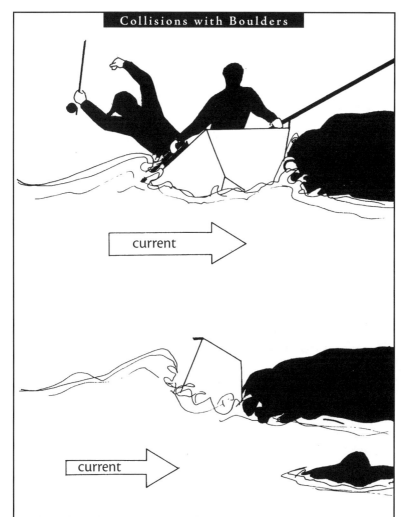

Collisions with Boulders

current

current

When a boat slams into a river-washed boulder, a predictable sequence of events can rapidly follow. The greater the speed and force of the water, the more likely the boat is to flip or wrap. The impact can be more jarring than you'd expect. Gear and people can fly overboard. Water instantly begins heaving up and possibly over the upstream side. This tends to shove it under the surface, possibly pinning the craft to the rock beneath tons of moving water. Although a boat can flip the other way, most flip and wrap with the hull side to the rock. Luckier craft just bounce and spin off, some half full of water.

The biggest danger in slamming into boulders is that rafts or drift boats can be flipped or wrapped. Rafts are more forgiving than drift boats in this regard and are preferred by many novice floaters as the best all-purpose craft. A river will apply tons of water pressure to a boat that's wrapped around the upstream side of a boulder. Often it's impossible to get the boat back off without a lot of extra manual or mechanical help. Many boats are abandoned as total losses in such situations, along with much of the equipment aboard. It's possible for people to get pinned between the boat and rock, too, drowning them. This doesn't seem to happen as often as it might, considering the abundant number of wrapped boats.

It's often necessary to seek help in removing a wrapped boat. Extra people, long ropes, winches, or even a motor vehicle might be needed to dislodge a craft from the current's grip. There are a few other tricks of the trade that we'll look at shortly, too. In some cases you might not be able to free the boat until the river drops a little. Hard-hull drift boats often buckle, collapsing around boulders. Rafts are more likely to be rescued intact due to their flexibility but can suffer damages to their tubes, floors, and rowing frames.

Wraps usually see panicked anglers floating and struggling downstream, scurrying to round up and save as much equipment as possible, and frequently suffering cuts and bruises as well as hypothermia in cold water and weather. On long-mileage river expeditions, such situations spell total disaster. You might have to hike out a canyon for miles to reach the nearest ranch (and many ranchers are not overfond of floaters to begin with) or depend on the generosity of other floaters to pick you up and take your party out. This could ruin *their* long-planned yearly river vacation, too. Experienced river runners are not always thrilled to bail out novices who get in over their heads, especially if being underequipped or underskilled was a major factor in the emergency. Serious first-aid can be an hour or two away at minimum, and sometimes an entire day.

When a boat plows into a boulder, the following sequence of events usually unfolds.

A sudden jolt sends equipment flying and can knock people out of their seats. The impact can be harder than imagined. Very often people in the boat will lean away from the rock in fear, which, as we'll

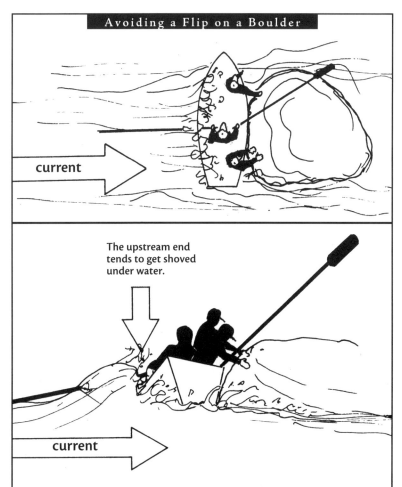

Avoiding a Flip on a Boulder

current

The upstream end tends to get shoved under water.

current

Once seriously engaged, the rower continues to stroke like mad, trying to spin the boat off the rock. Leaning away from the rock in fear just before impact tends to increase the chances of a flip. Passengers should be consciously acting as human ballast in an effort to keep the boat from flipping: Whatever side is going down should bring movement by them to the high side. Their weight can keep a boat from flipping, though of course it doesn't guarantee it. The boat could be filling with water at this point, and rowing could be of little help. Don life jackets now if you haven't already done so.

see shortly, can be opposite what they need to do. Human nature often leads the inexperienced and unlearned to do the wrong things in moving-water situations.

The water that was plowing into the upstream side of the boulder is now surging against the upstream side of your boat. It tends to climb rapidly up and over it and start to shove it underwater. The heavier and faster the water, the quicker this will take place. If the passengers on board lean away from the rock in fear (a natural reaction), they just help to sink the upstream side of the boat all the quicker. At this point the boat could wrap around the rock, getting pinned there, or it might fill partially with water, bounce and spin off the rock, and continue down the river, either right side up or upside down. It's also possible in turbulent water for a boat to wrap so that passengers become pinned between boat and rock. This happens much less often and usually in rougher rivers with surging currents. It can take superhuman rescue efforts to retrieve those in such immediate peril, calling for split-second decision making and action.

What needs to be done when you find yourself about to be side-slammed into a boulder is to take whatever last-ditch evasive actions are possible, then to be ready to use human weight as ballast, counteracting the boat's tendency to roll, flip, and wrap. This takes quick and determined action, which is helped immensely by having been thought about beforehand.

Just before hitting the rock, try to get in a last strong oar stroke or two to get the boat going to one side or the other of the boulder as much as possible. In this way you're more likely to bounce and spin off the obstruction, rather than broadsiding it and wrapping. What most experienced boatmen will do is to continue using the upstream oar to make powerful levering sweeps, trying to spin the boat off the boulder before it starts to wrap. Some will even try to get a spin going on the boat before it hits the rock, hoping for a pinball deflection (which can be quite jolting).

Because boats usually end up pinned sideways to rocks, the downstream oar is likely to be wedged uselessly against the boulder or blown out of the oar lock and rendered inoperable. The upstream oar needs to be used with a vengeance to pry and spin the boat off the rock before it starts to fill with water and wrap.

At the same time, experienced floaters (or anglers) will know that the upstream side of the boat is likely to get shoved underwater, which causes the wrap or flip. What they'll instinctively do is lean into the rock, using their body weight as ballast in fighting the boat's tendency to be pushed under. Human ballast is an important aspect of white-water rowing. Even anglers might need to resort to it to save the boat and equipment in a pinch (because anglers don't expect flips and don't tie their equipment in).

Because water is pushing the upstream side of the boat down and underwater, the downstream side tends to be lifted a bit. It's here that human weight needs to be applied to counteract a flip. All the while the oarsman should continue to row like mad, trying to lever and spin the boat off one side or the other. Most often it will come free. In easy flows there might be no consequences. In heavier currents it's likely that the boat will have shipped a lot of water that will need to be bailed (unless you have a self-bailing raft). It can also roll over and flip before coming loose, which necessitates a major rehab operation. There may be equipment or people that got washed overboard to be rounded up. Broken oars are another possibility. Bringing extra oars, oar locks, patch kits, and first-aid kits along is a must for challenging rivers, along with a pump for rafts. In addition, life jackets, ropes, and a list of other equipment should be taken on every trip down a river. We'll look at this more closely in Chapter 6.

If the boat does wrap and stick, you have some quick decisions to make. You might want to round up as much equipment as possible before it floats downstream beyond recovery. Any serious injuries need to be dealt with and a rescue plan implemented. Hypothermia can be a real threat. Anyone routinely involved in outdoor sports should take first-aid and CPR classes at regular intervals.

The ability to pull a wrapped boat off a boulder can depend upon the possession of a long rope. This may need to be rescued from the wrapped boat before it can be used. The rope must be attached securely to the boat at the end that is most likely to free the wrap. This usually means that someone will have to go upstream a bit, then swim down to the raft, grab on, and tie the rope in place. This isn't always easy, safe, or possible. Freezing cold water is especially daunting and dangerous.

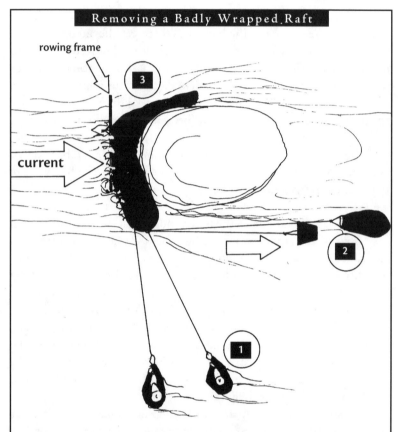

Removing a Badly Wrapped Raft

rowing frame

current

Wrapped rafts can be very difficult to pull off rocks.
1. Enough people pulling on long ropes can do the job, presuming you have ropes along.
2. Buckets and other gear can be hung off ropes and straps for added pull in the current.
3. Deflating one side of the raft, or even cutting the floor open on one side, might be necessary to loosen the river's grip on the boat. This would depend on your ability to get back out to the raft, of course.

Even getting the rope attached doesn't mean that three people can pull the boat off a boulder. A strong current can apply several tons of pressure due to the water heaving against it. If the boat is but lightly balanced on the rock, it might come off with a few serious pulls. If another boating party drifts by, enlist their aid, too. It could take a dozen or more people to do the job. Of course, if you don't carry a 50-foot heavy-duty rope for such occasions, you'll just be standing there dripping wet with a blank stare on your face. Few anglers go forth with the same precautions with which serious white-water boaters do, because flipping isn't in their game plan. Being rescue-equipped, however, isn't a bad idea, even if you know your river. The river gods always seem to come up with new ways to test your skills, equipment, and vehicles!

There are a few other ploys to use with rafts. These also rely on your being able to get back to your boat and wrestle (literally) with the problem. Deflating one-half of the raft can loosen the river's grip, making it easier to pull the inflated side off. Some boaters have tied ropes to the inflated end and connected to them buckets, waterproof bags, or whatever else might be on hand. These items drag downstream in the current, adding more pull. This can be critical when human helpers are in short supply. In some cases boaters will slit the raft floor at one end, allowing water to pour through the raft, which lessens the wrapping effect. These added efforts, plus enough force on the rope, can free a badly wrapped boat. Though repairs are likely to be needed, at least you have a boat to continue on with.

A wrapped drift boat gives you fewer options, for even more water weight is likely to be holding it in place. On the other hand, a drift boat's hull is more curved, allowing it to be rocked and pulled off boulders easily at times. Its floor, too, is more slippery than a raft's. In some cases the hull will collapse around a rock, leaving the boat a near total loss.

If you leave a boat wrapped around a rock and walk out, it's your responsibility to go back with help and get it off later, perhaps when the water level has dropped a bit. It's just river garbage now, and you are guilty of littering! Besides, there's almost always equipment of value to be salvaged. There are even experts at river-boat salvage because of the frequency with which expensive boats are wrapped and sunk on some of the more powerful western steelhead and trout rivers that flow to the Pacific.

HOLES

When water pours over the top of barely submerged boulders, it creates what's known as a hole in white-water circles. This is of course completely different from a fishing hole. The presence and intensity of holes vary in differing water levels. At low water a boulder might be poking high above the surface and need to be rowed around. At medium to high water the river could be covering the boulder, creating a strong suck hole behind it. At flood stage there could be a vicious boat-flipping hole in the same place. With enough water, both boulder and hole will submerge. You might see only a series of standing waves in their place.

When a river pours over a boulder or ledge, the weight and inertia of the quick-flowing water forces the main current down toward the bottom of the river. The water right behind the rock near the surface rushes back upstream to fill the void. This results in a turbulent backflow capable of flipping boats in the blink of an eye. The bigger and wider the hole and the greater the volume of water and distance it drops, the greater its effect on boats. A small boulder's hole can be easily "punched through" by a rowed craft. You can even park there, letting the sucking effect hold the boat in place. A big drop over a larger boulder or river-wide ledge can pose serious flip potential, especially to novices. Holes that don't look or sound bad can give the Maytag treatment to the unexpecting!

What usually happens when a boat drops over a rock or ledge into a big hole is as follows. The boat speeds up a bit as it plunges over the drop in a quickening current. When the boat hits the big hole it's slammed to an immediate halt by the turbulence that's rushing back upstream. This jolt alone can throw people and equipment from the boat in severe cases, so passengers should be holding on! If the forward (downstream) inertia of the boat doesn't push it through the turbulence and downstream, it will usually get spun sideways by the backflow and shoved upstream into the hole, just behind the rock. Here the water rushing down and over the boulder will fill and shove the upstream side of the boat under water. The turbulence pushing

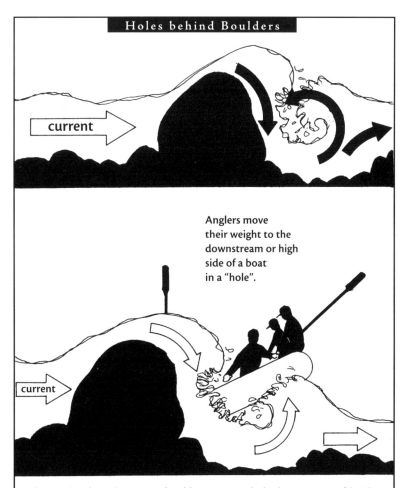

Holes behind Boulders

current

Anglers move
their weight to the
downstream or high
side of a boat
in a "hole".

current

River water dropping over a boulder creates a hole downstream of it. The weight and velocity of the water dropping over the rock pushes its downstream current below the river's surface. A strong upstream surge of water fills this void. Boats caught here are spun sideways and are likely to be flipped by the down-and-up force of the hole. Rowing to escape and using human ballast are important in avoiding flips. Boats often spin around and around in big holes, so passengers must be alert to the boat's position in the hole, moving themselves accordingly to counteract the boat's tendency to flip. The part of the boat closest to the hole-producing rock is the side that will be shoved under.

up from the downstream side helps push that side up and over. This double whammy by a powerhouse hole can flip a boat so fast that you won't know what hit you. The panicked look on floaters' faces in this rapid-fire progression is somewhat comical, but there is real danger posed to those involved in the incident.

Even if the boat doesn't flip, it's likely to be held in the hole for a while and fill with water. The upstream-pushing turbulence constantly wants to shove the boat back into the heart of the hole. As it gains hundreds of pounds in shipped water, the boat is more likely to be washed out of the hole, though it then becomes much harder to effectively row.

What needs to be done here is to use passenger body weight again as ballast. Once you are in a hole and quickly realize that the water pouring over the boulder is likely to roll and flip your boat, you need to move your weight to the downstream end or side of the craft to counteract that force. This can require the immediate action of everyone in the boat and probably a stern commander yelling the proper moves to stem disaster and panic.

The rower's oars will likely be temporarily out of commission, because boats tend to be swung sideways and pushed up tight behind the boulder when in a hole. The turbulence and proximity of the rock can make rowing at this point very difficult, yet the boatman should continue trying to row his way out of the hole. The rest of the crew needs to be using their weight as ballast to avoid a flip and should remain alert to the boat's position in the hole. Boats will slowly rotate in holes. You'll need to move bodies around to whatever is the downstream end of the boat as it rotates, remaining conscious of what's transpiring. The rower will be doing whatever he can with the oars but may also have to throw his weight around in critical moments. Drift boats will be less forgiving in holes: They lack the inherent flotation of rafts. Human ballast will be of even greater concern, and many drift boats will simply sink. Many have no flotation other than trapped air in storage compartments.

The water pouring over the boulder usually pours into the boat as well. This can wash unsecured equipment (and people) downstream. Once the boat fills with water, it's less likely to flip, though giant holes can flip anything. The boat's partially sunken weight tends to catch the deeper-flowing current that moves downstream. Eventually it flounders out of the hole.

Holes can hold boats for a few seconds or for a minute or more. This depends on the size and shape of the hole, the drop, and the force of the water. A hole behind a narrow rock isn't likely to hold your boat very long, though it could possibly flip it, then send you on your merry way downstream. A big wide boulder (say 10–20 feet wide) or a wide ledge drop could hold you for quite a while. Boats can be flipped and rolled numerous times in killer holes and bashed around for several minutes. Often floaters will be knocked out of the boat, wash free, and drift downstream while their raft continues to circulate. This is due to the raft's greater buoyancy and tendency to be held in the hole. A drift boat generally fills with water and sinks, getting washed out of the hole in less time. A sunk boat going down the river is likely to get beat up, though, or pinned deep against a rock. It can be very hard to regain possession of.

Not having a life jacket on can be disastrous for anyone not mentally and physically up to swimming in turbulent and possibly frigid water. In frothing white water and especially in holes, a person's head will be under water as much or more than above, even when wearing a life jacket. The vertically circulating water in a hole spins you round and round. You often come back up to the surface under the boat, too, and have to scramble to get from beneath it for a gasp of air. If all this sounds disconcerting, then I'm making my point. You have to be alert enough to keep your eyes open and see when your head is above water to take a breath. Circulating in a nasty hole is very disorienting, too. A quick spin and ejection from a hole will scare you a bit. A prolonged experience will scare the hell out of you. As soon as you are ejected, shaking from adrenalin and cold water, you have to be conscious enough to help others in your party, or at least start gathering up floating gear, as well as drag out the boat itself.

Although white-water enthusiasts prepare for flips by wearing life jackets (and even wet suits and helmets) and carrying safety and throw ropes, anglers generally do not. White-water floaters might even enjoy a flip if they're experienced. Float fishermen just tend to panic, lose equipment, and occasionally drown.

The thing to do with holes is avoid them. On most fishing waters holes are easily missed with enough foresight and the proper rowing skills. If you spy a big hump of water that looks like a rounded up-heave and you can't see over it or what's downstream behind it, it's probably a hole. You'll often be going down a concentrated chute filled with growing waves. Suddenly you see a wave that's bigger than the rest with dead quiet water just downstream of it—the hole. Being up-river blocks your view of many holes. They're hidden behind the up-surge of water as it goes over the rock. The distance water falls over a clean ledge drop can hide the view of the turbulent hole itself in that case. You'll often hear the roar before seeing the roll-back wave. In some cases ledge drops are hard to see coming because the quiet flow upstream of the drop and the quiet water just downstream of the tur-bulent hole blend together, giving an illusion of a continuous stretch of flat water. If you hear a roar but see nothing, it's time to quickly make for the bank, get out of the boat, and scout out the situation. Any time you see a piece of flat water ahead in the midst of concen-trated currents and waves, it's likely a rock and its hole are causing it.

Be alert and row around holes. When ferrying across a river, don't row in just behind big holes. They can actually suck you back upstream and flip you just as sure as if you came down over them. Ferry behind such boulders where the water flattens out and has no appreciable upstream sucking flow. This is especially true with clean wide ledge drops and manmade diversion dams, which can have amazing upstream tow and hole holding power, even when they don't look particularly dangerous.

If you are going to hit a big hole, make sure everybody puts on life jackets, secures what gear they can, and holds on tight. Hitting a hole head-on can be jolting. What the rower needs to do, once hitting a hole is deemed unavoidable, is build up as much downstream speed as possible. You want to blow through that heavy upstream-surging turbulence and push the boat downstream beyond its reversed flow. (Holes are also known as "reversals.") If you see it coming early enough and can't avoid it, you might want to turn the boat quickly around and back row downstream. This gives you more power and downstream speed both before you hit the hole and when you're in it. Don't try to spin the boat into the reverse position just as you're drop-ping into the hole, though, because being sideways to the hole is what

A V slot, as seen here, often identifies the proper chute to aim for. Boat-eating holes can be located just to the sides of such Vs. Big waves requiring some quick maneuvering are likely after a boat slides down the V chute and into the turbulence below.

you want to avoid most. If you find yourself suddenly face to face with a big hole, just row forward as hard and fast as you can to build maximum downstream inertia. Try your best to blast through.

Once in the hole, a boatman should row like mad to keep that downstream momentum going and to keep from getting spun sideways and sucked back into the drop. With enough downstream inertia and speed you can power through small and medium-sized holes. Monster holes are likely to eat you no matter what. They can flip even big boats end over end or, as often happens, spin boats sideways, suck them in, and roll them over and over. Part of your prefloat research should include pinpointing the location of any river hazards. There are detailed maps of most rivers available these days that identify dangers.

When a raft drops into a big hole it can buckle and almost fold in half. Serious white-water floaters will make sure their boats are pumped tight to avoid this buckling effect. There have been cases of people's arms or legs getting trapped between the rowing frame and raft as the boat folds, only to be wedged there when it straightens

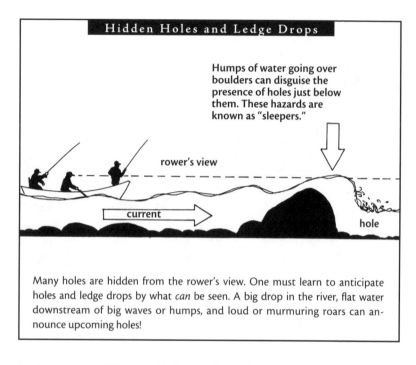

Hidden Holes and Ledge Drops

Humps of water going over boulders can disguise the presence of holes just below them. These hazards are known as "sleepers."

rower's view

current

hole

Many holes are hidden from the rower's view. One must learn to anticipate holes and ledge drops by what *can* be seen. A big drop in the river, flat water downstream of big waves or humps, and loud or murmuring roars can announce upcoming holes!

back out—possibly upside down after a flip in the hole. Limbs have been broken and floaters knocked unconscious in these situations. People drown every year in big holes, ledges, and diversion dams. These are extreme cases but nevertheless realities of floating strong rivers and missing the proper channels and chutes. Drift boats are less forgiving than rafts in most white-water situations because they don't have the same flotation qualities and can flip rather quickly. On the other hand, they usually row better and respond quicker to oar strokes. Whatever you row, treat big holes with plenty of respect.

Ledges and Diversion Dams

Holes are taken a step further when water pours over a clean drop ledge or manmade diversion dam. Here the suction and flip effect of a hole can occur on a river-wide, inescapable scale. Even what appear to be short-drop diversion dams create some strong all-consuming holes that don't look turbulent. Such holes are stronger than

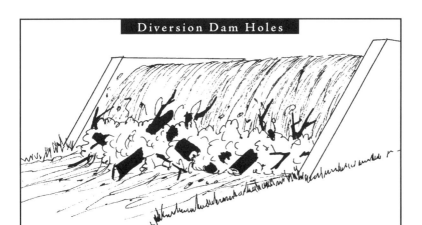

Diversion Dam Holes

Some diversion dams have rather innocent-looking but powerful bank-to-bank holes. Rotating debris in the vortex indicates a hole that doesn't like to let its objects go! This could include humans in life jackets. Avoid diversion-dam holes—portage around them. Some natural rock ledges have equally threatening and near-river-wide holes. Some killer holes may be identified on floaters' maps, but not all!

they appear. Though some can be rowed through with enough forward speed, many claim lives on a yearly basis. It's their innocent look matched with an unrelenting backwash that gets floaters and swimmers in trouble.

If you see sticks and flotsam sucked in and circulating just behind the drop of a straight-edged ledge or dam, take that as a serious hint that this hole doesn't like to let its possessions go! Some diversion dams will hold debris for weeks!

Although broken ledges can have slots to aim for where navigable chutes pour through, river-wide ledges and dams should be scouted and portaged if any doubts occur. It's not worth flipping a boat and losing gear and possibly lives to pamper the ego of a novice or ignorant rower.

Logjams

Sweepers (fallen trees) and logjams can present greater dangers than boulders in many cases. Water bounces off and deflects around

Logjam Danger

Whereas water must bounce off and go around individual boulders, it can sift through logjams without losing much speed. A boat or swimming angler pinned in a logjam can be in a serious, even life-threatening, situation.

boulders. Logjams, on the other hand (also called "strainers") allow water to run through them. A boat or body can be pinned among the trunks and sharp limbs with a force beyond retrieval. The limbs can puncture raft tubes, even on glancing blows. Getting shoved into a logjam should be avoided at all costs. Portage a totally choked stretch of river if need be, and scout any channel in question.

Individual logs and jams can move from year to year. Early-season high and dropping river flows call for great caution. Once rivers settle into summer lows, channels usually become established around most logjams through erosion. Other floaters and Fish and Game departments often chain saw bad ones out of the way on more popular rivers. If you are on a long expedition on a known logjammed river, it wouldn't hurt to carry a small chain saw. It's easier than doing a major portage with lots of heavy gear.

Nonetheless, channels through many logjams can be narrow, requiring precise rowing. Protruding logs will be there to interfere with

Tight squeezes between boulders and logs are common occurrences, especially on smaller backcountry rivers. Having the judgment and skill to navigate them can mean the difference between a safe journey and a punctured raft or flipped drift boat.

some critical oar strokes. I find the crawl stroke to be most useful in some of these situations, because it allows me to pass obstacles more closely on the sweep-oar side. A novice shouldn't depend on the crawl stroke, however, until it and its limitations are perfectly understood.

Stop and scout bends in rivers where the full force of the current seems to plow into what appears as a river-wide logjam. Though there will usually be a path through it, knowing the route beforehand can eliminate apprehension and possible misjudgment. These are often tight fits. As with all maneuvering, the preplanning of your route and set-up are very important here. The ability to make quick decisions, instant turns, and last-second maneuvers needs to become second nature.

River Bends

As rivers go around sharp bends, the force of the current usually concentrates, pushing water into the outside bank of the bend. It often picks up speed here and can build up compression waves due to a more restricted and concentrated flow. Water that's squeezed in a narrow swift channel wants to go somewhere. It tends to go up, building into taller waves, which are ultimately held in check by gravity. (When that compressed water suddenly gets the chance to spread back out laterally, it can create strong whirlpools in big side eddies or behind boulders.) There are some river waves in excess of 20 feet. As water sprawls across the tailout of a river beyond the bend, it tends to spread out and flatten, with gravity smearing it across a widened bed.

As the water rushes around the outside bend, it both erodes it and tends to lodge some boulders and logs there. The bank along an outside bend is often steep. Boulders get exposed or rolled into place here, either from being pushed by water and ice over the years, or from rolling down the eroded hillside. In either case it's not unusual to find the outside of a bend littered with boulders, rocks, and perhaps a log or two. The inside bend, on the other hand, is usually composed of finer sands, gravel, or cobble. The eddy there, known as the eye of the pool, is slower and circulates horizontally, allowing finer silts and sands to drop out of the current (and trout to hold there). The heavy

Maneuvering Around Sharp River Bends

outside of bend

inside of bend

current

Direction the stern points during back rowing.

A rower approaching a sharp bend in a river should anticipate having to row away from the outside of the bend before actually getting into it. The boat should be pivoted well in advance. Some crosscurrent inertia toward the inside bend must be gained before the boat gets into the corner. Currents will tend to shove the boat into the outside-bend bank, where tumbled boulders and logjams left by floods can further complicate maneuvering. Pull over early to scout if blind corners, steep drops, logjams, or loud roars greet you on a sharp bend.

currents on the swifter banks keep those silts moving, allowing only heavy rocks to settle and not get pushed any farther downstream. Until the next ice jam or flood, that is.

Because the current can be expected to push a boat toward the outside bend, you'll want to angle your stern *crosscurrent* a bit, aiming it toward the inside bend of the river before you actually get into the corner. River currents are not always parallel with the banks, so be alert to the direction of the current, not just to the banks. You also need to begin making some stronger oar strokes to get some back-ferrying momentum built up before entering the corner itself. Once you have a back-rowing head of steam, the proper back-ferrying angle, and correct entry set-up, negotiating bends becomes easier. There can be big boulders to dodge, both in the chute and along the steeper, swifter bank. Be alert for these. Rocks, holes, and logjams can all be found along sharp bends. They require an extra level of awareness and preparedness in order to make quick decisions and take evasive action.

Where beginners get into trouble is when they let themselves be pushed too far into the outside bend before beginning to back away from it. If nothing else, this tends to cut into the fishing potential if the boat is shoved right up against a bank. The bankside oar can be rendered useless by the shore's proximity until the boat is pivoted into the proper ferrying angle to get away from it. This will be harder now, because the full force of the current is driving the boat into the bank. Collisions with boulders and logs are common, too, when beginners fail to ferry away from a corner before getting right into it. These are prime locations to wrap a boat or flip in a hole. Damage can be done to boats and equipment can be lost when the craft side slams even minor rocks or logs.

If you will recall the discussion of the crawl stroke in Chapter 2, it, too, can be used to round corners if they're not too demanding. I usually use a combination of the back stroke and the crawl when rounding corners, endeavoring to keep a smooth rowing pace and even track so anglers aren't jostled and can capitalize on this fish-producing zone. If your float time allows, it's a good idea to row around the bend, pull over, anchor or tie off a little way down the run, and come back upstream to wade-fish the eye of the pool, eddy line, and perhaps systematically nymph the drop-off leading into them. If you can reach the far side, it's usually sprinkled with fish-holding pockets among the larger rocks found there and is well worth pursuing. It could be more productive to drop an angler off on that side at the tail of the run, then go anchor on the other side and let the second angler go up the inside bend. In that way both sides as well as the middle of the river are covered most thoroughly.

Reading and Clearing Rapids

Although running very technical white water is beyond the scope of this book, it does every boater good to get some white-water experience to hone rowing skills. There are plenty of great fishing rivers with well-known rapids. Most rapids are an intensification of water speed, river drop, channelization, sharp turns, and boulder congestion. The ability to read water, set up, make quick decisions, and carry them out becomes critical in white water. Turbulence and waves can make getting a good oar plant trickier at times. The need for pivot turns and power back ferries can come fast and furiously. There can be holes that eat boats in a blink of an eye. The basic required maneuvers are the same, but the more powerful water pushes you harder, testing your skills and strength. A couple of missed oar strokes due to water turbulence or a faulty read can end in a collision, spill, or wrap.

Types of rapids vary, largely due to bedrock formations rivers flow through in addition to the residual effects of landslides, which drop some huge boulders into rivers along steeply eroded slopes. Any combination of elements can be found. Some rivers tend to have fairly straightforward pool-drop-run sequences. A few have boulder gardens and big standing waves for miles on end. The latter aren't run for fishing much but are mostly white-water playgrounds (though many do have good fishing at low flows). Because we're most interested in fishing applications and generally mellower rivers, we'll discuss some of these added hazards briefly, not wallowing around too long in the rapids.

ROCK OR BOULDER GARDENS

"Rock garden" is a white-water term for a boulder-studded reach of river. Many are caused by rock slides off steep hillsides or avalanche chutes. Over the centuries (and one really does float through time, geologically speaking, on a river), accumulated rock slides can fill a section of river with big boulders. These occur most on outside bends of the river, where a steep bank continually erodes. These areas create challenging runs, the kind white-water enthusiasts thrive on. Adrenalin rushes seem to be as addictive as rising trout. There are many famous rapids that were caused by rock slides. Avalanches, heavy rain

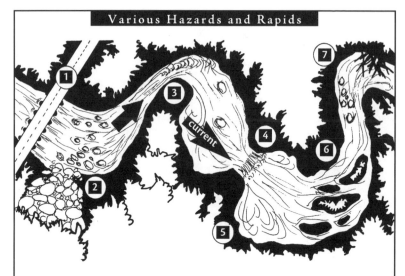

Various Hazards and Rapids

1. Bridge pilings with narrow slots and low bridges.
2. Boulder gardens, often caused by landslides off steep hillsides.
3. Large compression waves caused by a narrowing chute intensified by a steeper drop. Side curlers rolling off cliff walls and serious holes are likely, too. Powerhouse whirlpools can occur when the water has a chance to spread back out. This is a typical gorge scenario.
4. Ledge drops and manmade diversion dams can create bad holes.
5. Strong whirlpools where rivers widen are particularly strong at high water.
6. Narrow, congested channels in island systems. Watch for logjams.
7. Blind corners can lead into rapids and logjams. If in doubt, scout!

and erosion, floods, ice jams, and earthquakes all can create and re-arrange rapids.

Many boulder gardens call for scouting. A deep roar and unclear channel should lead you to the bank. The boat is beached *well* up-stream of the rapid, so that upon reembarking you have the rowing room to set up properly anywhere across the river. After beaching, crew members walk downstream to explore and memorize the different possible rowing routes. The best route is chosen and its landmarks noted. Things will look a lot different once you are out in the water, however. Sometimes, in a very technical piece of water, the boatman might opt to take the boat through alone. Reducing the human weight by several hundred pounds does make a difference in the ease of rowing. On the other hand, a heavier boat doesn't usually flip as easily, especially if everyone on board knows how to use their weight as ballast. There might be party members who physically wouldn't be up to any mishaps or a nasty swim through the rapids. Some people have an undeniable fear of big churning water, too. Such party members will feel a lot safer walking around threatening rapids. No amount of cajoling will have much effect on this state of mind, though going through a progression of river trips from easy to moderate and finally to challenging can lessen the fear of water, along with a good understanding of how water acts and is dealt with. There are quite a few people who love to fish yet have a fear of moving water.

In any case, after scouting the rapid, life jackets are tightened, equipment is tied in, and the crew is readied for any eventuality. Using your body weight as ballast can be critical on a white-water run in a smaller fishing craft. Having identified the best route, the rower tries to memorize the boulder sequence and his upcoming maneuvers much like a downhill ski racer memorizes his course. Knowing your route ahead of time is of great advantage when split-second decision making is needed and surging currents make some oar strokes a lot less effective than you hoped they'd be.

Once the rapid has been entered, all maneuvering is done with strong back strokes—never forward ones. The crawl stroke isn't strong enough for big-water work; quick pivots and power ferries are likely to be needed. Eddies behind big boulders can be used to help slow the boat down and cross over to different current lanes. Don't pull in too closely and get sucked back up into a hole! Big holes are to be feared and avoided. If you are headed for one (and there are plenty of cases where big holes are unavoidable), increase your downstream speed in hopes of blasting through it. If you're sucked back into it, remain very alert. Use your body weight to counteract flips. You may at times have to spin the boat completely around in a tight maneuver between boulders. I have fun doing this occasionally in a calculated rock-squeezing fashion, using the eddies behind to help suck me in and spin back around. Naturally you'll want anglers to have their fly lines in when performing such maneuvers. A skilled crew, though, can have fun fishing their way through a rapid if it is not overwhelming.

Such stretches don't see much fishing pressure. Pockets will need to be covered fast, but the fish can be just as fast at grabbing your fly. Swift-water rivers often breed gung ho trout.

You may encounter boulder gardens that are either too narrow to even squeeze a boat through or so powerful that your better judgment elects not to run them. In these cases you must either portage your boat and equipment around the rapid, or line through, tied to a long rope(s). A boat minus its human cargo weight can often be slid over shallow spots you couldn't otherwise float through. In heavy-water spots you might want to wrap your end of the rope around a rock or tree to snub the boat. Otherwise, the potential could be there for the boat to pull you into the water. Boulder gardens and rapids often call for intelligent decisions and contingency plans.

Many of the rock gardens I encounter in midsummer have lots of boulders but not very powerful flows. Fishing is good in these places. You'll want to row here as smoothly as possible, putting anglers in the best position you can. The crawl stroke again becomes a most useful ploy, reducing excess pivot turns and ferries to minimums. One still has to be cautious, though. It's possible to wrap boats around rocks in fairly insignificant flows if you do everything wrong!

STANDING WAVES

Ocean waves move, rolling in toward the coast. River waves stay relatively still—the water moves through them. In rapids these are often called standing waves. They're usually caused by the narrowing of a river channel or the concentration of an accelerating current down a chute. River waves are sometimes referred to as "compression waves."

On smaller scales there's not much to worry about. Many chutes with smaller standing waves are deep, with few or no rocks to dodge. Always be alert, though, boulders or logs could still be hidden within. When waves start getting more than 3–4 feet high, it's time to be on your toes. Here, too, many chutes with compression waves are deep and have no obstacles to dodge. There are, however, many chutes and rapids with big waves that are also boulder-studded or have sudden ledge drops. Seeing obstacles ahead becomes more difficult, because tall waves obscure your forward view. When down in the trough between two waves you might not be able to see anything except the top of the next wave. It's when your boat rides the crests of waves that you want to scan very carefully ahead for hidden boulders, ledges, and killer holes. In a deep straightforward chute, the waves will be regularly spaced and similar in height. The boat trip through will be like a roller-coaster ride. In a more complex rapid, irregular, extra tall and back-curling waves, side curlers, and sudden flat spots in the channel ahead can indicate the presence of boulders, ledges, logs, and holes. You might even need to stand up in your boat briefly to get a better view over the waves and chart your course. Again, you may want to scout any rapid in question before committing to run it. You'll want to be ready to make instant decisions, quick pivot turns, and powerful back strokes.

Even if you give a boulder a glancing blow, the water that heaves off its upstream side will tend to shove your boat away from it at the last second. During a last-ditch evasion this might send you into a spin from which you'll quickly need to right yourself. In big water, back-curling waves breaking off a large boulder can be big enough to flip boats that go into them sideways. Your maneuvering now must also concern itself with wave height and turbulence. Pivot and back row when you can, but spin your boat nose-first into big back curlers, waves, and holes when the threat of a flip is real. This is often done at the very last second.

The bigger waves get, the greater concern they cause. River waves of 6 feet in height are quite common. Ten- to 15-foot waves can be found on many white-water rivers and on some popular fishing rivers in flood. There are even waves of 15–30 feet on a few waters, monster waves of renown.

When waves get beyond a certain height, they often form back curlers, similar in look to those breaking on an ocean beach. These can be turbulent enough to flip boats that go into them sideways, or at least will fill them with a lot of water. Small rafts can even "surf" on giant waves and can slide back down the wave into the trough if the wave is tall enough and the raft's forward motion is stalled. The back-curling wave can then keep breaking onto the boat, flushing it with water. Boats half full of water weigh an immense amount, thousands of pounds. Rowing that kind of additional weight around doesn't get you very far! This is one reason self-bailing rafts (and even drift boats) have become popular in white-water circles. Rafts filled with water are largely at the river's mercy. A boater's control of them is minimal.

With the right bottom configuration or channelization, it's easy for big waves to evolve into holes. A series of big standing waves with back curlers might drop over just a bit of a ledge or big boulder, which suddenly confronts you with a flip-worthy hole.

The trick is to hit big back-curling waves nose-on. Avoid getting into them sideways. This can call for the repeated pivoting of the boat, both for maneuvering and to hit big waves nose-on. Due to the nature of compression waves, they often break at 45-degree angles, coming from both sides of the river. You might have to swing your nose into the crest of each really big wave, just at the last second, first right, then left, back right, and so on. Sometimes maneuvering becomes an absolute must. Consequently, some big waves have to be broadsided to some degree. This is another case where using human cargo as ballast can be important. If a big wave starts to flip your boat over sideways, your crew needs to throw their body weight into the high side in an attempt to knock it back down and avoid a flip. This becomes something like throwing a football body block in extreme cases. It's not unusual to find yourself occasionally thrown to the floor of the boat. It is necessary to stay aware of the boat's position in the water and to adjust the human ballast in order to keep the craft upright. Extreme case, yes. But it happens frequently on numerous trout and steelhead rivers.

In steep-walled canyons and along some sharp river bends, big waves can break as they pile up against the banks. Such waves can be irregular and surging, angling off the walls at about 45-degree angles. Many such waves can be totally avoided with the proper set-up and advance back ferrying. The current, though, will be trying to shove you into the wall. If you let the river push you too far, you'll have to both angle your boat sharply away from the outside bend wall as well as pivot the bow of your boat to hit big back curlers head-on. You might have to maneuver and back row like mad in the troughs of the waves and swing the nose back around for every big breaking crest. In a poorly controlled craft it's possible for the water to shove it right into the wall, where an oar can be incapacitated or broken. This leaves you temporarily at the river's mercy, and some *big* waves, boulders, and holes are likely to be

Side Curlers

current

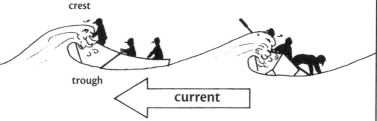

crest

trough

current

Big side curlers rolling off cliff walls and boulders can flip small fishing craft. Avoid them when possible or hit them bow-first, not sideways. Sometimes a serious evasive rowing maneuver may make it necessary to broadside a big back curler or hole. If so, use your human ballast to counteract any boat-flipping tendencies, and row like mad!

just downstream! This is a typical flip scenario. Pardon the repetition, but early recognition, set-up, and preliminary back-ferrying momentum are the keys to staying out of trouble here.

Once you get the feel of running more challenging water and get some white-water experience, you'll have a lot of fun at the oars. A mix of good fishing with some stretches of moderate white water makes for an enjoyable day. The diversity keeps your mind alert as you drift through beautiful canyons and valleys. The sights, sounds, and river-scented breezes make a special chemistry craved by all river addicts.

SWIMMING AND SELF-RESCUE IN RAPIDS

The time-honored method of swimming through a rapid, rock garden, or other area of swift water depends upon a high-quality, type 5 life jacket and the defensive positioning of the backstroke. Type 5 life jackets (a government standard) are highly buoyant, with a collar that theoretically keeps the wearer's head above water, even if the wearer is unconscious. Consider the term white water. It's rushing, tumbling water that appears white because it's infused with air bubbles. The whiter it is, the more air is churned into it, and the less you float! Your buoyancy goes down as air infusion goes up, even with a life jacket. Add to this the down-pulling currents of a hole, crashing back curler, or whirlpool, and the need for a life jacket becomes obvious. No knowledgeable boater, even the best, thinks of running a white-water stretch without a life jacket.

On the whole, anglers tend not to wear life jackets because they restrict movement. Anglers wear fishing vests and usually have a degree of faith in their guide or boatman. However, life jackets are required aboard most watercraft by law in most states. Anglers should put them on whenever facing water they wouldn't feel comfortable swimming through, especially if their rower is a novice.

The swimming backstroke position confers three advantages: The swimmer can see where he is headed downstream; he can use feet and hands to fend off rocks; at the same time, he can backstroke toward shore, using a 45-degree ferrying angle that he'd use if rowing. An angler who gets washed or dumped out of a boat can usually just swim back to it unless separated from the boat by swirling whirlpools and currents. It's decidedly tougher to reenter a boat when wearing a life jacket, though, especially if also encumbered by waders, a jacket, and what have you. It can be necessary for the rest of the crew to drag a swimmer back on board while also navigating tricky water. Any swimmer hanging on to the outside of a boat that's still going through rough water should avoid being on the downstream end or side of the boat, where a collision with a rock could put the swimmer between the two.

Don't try to stand up in swift boulder-studded water. There's a chance your feet can get stuck between rocks and wedged there. If this happens, the current will knock you over. With an anchored foot you'll be flattened by the river and very possibly shoved underwater. Drownings, even of people wearing high-quality life jackets, happen this way from time to time. Instead of trying to stand once you've fallen in, immediately assume the backstroke position, keeping your feet near the water surface. Look for the boat or nearest safe bank and start backstroking there at a ferrying angle. Don't stand up until you reach slower shallow water, where getting your foot snagged would be unlikely.

An angler wearing waders and no life jacket faces a more serious swim. If the waders are baggy at all, they'll balloon out a bit when the wearer backstrokes against the current, causing noticeable and unwanted drag. You might want to swim more sideways to the current or a little down and across in this case, because then the current will have less effect on your waders. Do keep your eyes open, though. Pick a swimming route and prepare to use feet and hands to fend off rocks while using the backstroke. There is a "pillow" that surrounds rocks caused by the water moving around them. It will usually lessen physical impact with the rocks. Tightly clustered boulders act like sieves, however, and should be avoided if possible.

When swimming through big waves, expect your head to go under water through the crest of each wave. It will reemerge once you're heading down into the next trough. It's very important to keep your eyes open so that you know when to breathe and where to swim. There are many turbulences that will submerge your head at times, even if you are wearing the best life jacket. Wave crests and breakers, holes, and whirlpools can all temporarily push or suck you under. You must see opportunities to breathe or hold your breath as

Swimming in Rapids

If you do get washed out of a boat in heavy water, immediately assume a back-stroking position, assess your situation, and back ferry toward the boat or near-est safe shore. Use your feet and hands to fend off boulders. Don't try to stand up until you've reached slow shallow water. When going through big waves, ex-pect your head to go under the water in the crests. Keep your eyes open and your mind alert. Breathe in the troughs when your head resurfaces. Hold your breath in the crests, holes, and whenever you see that you're about to go under. Always wear a life jacket in strong water.

long as necessary. If you don't keep your eyes open and your mind alert you'll be at much greater risk. Try not to panic if you fall in the river. Immediately sum up your and the boat's position, formulate a plan of self-rescue, and implement it using the backstroke.

If you've never fallen into ice-cold water, be aware of its effects. First, it will make you gasp for breath, sometimes uncontrollably. Not being able to choose moments of breathing when swimming through rough water is an added danger. You can become numb and half-para-lyzed in a very short period of time, sometimes even less than a minute. The better the shape you're in (with little body fat), the quicker you can be affected by the cold. Soon you'll have a hard time effectively swimming or grabbing onto bankside rocks to save yourself. Before very long your thinking will become disoriented; you won't even care much about what's going on. Hypothermia sets in fast. This is a real danger in the early season when rivers can be high and icy cold. Late-season trips carry the hypothermia threat, too, though most rivers are low and clear then. People even get hypothermia in midsummer, during cold wind- and rainstorms. Some rivers below big dams never warm up much.

One good feature of modern neoprene waders is that they give an added degree of flotation and insulation, should you take a swim. Most are snug-fitting too, so ballooning with water isn't a big problem. The insulating factor can be very important.

Early and late in the season, extricating yourself from the river doesn't end your troubles, because cold air temperatures and wind only heighten the hypothermic effect. A fire could be an absolute necessity, along with a change of clothes. This is one reason polypropylene clothes are so popular with floaters and anglers. Their water-repelling properties make them a top insulating choice. You can wring and whip most of the water from a polypropylene garment and it will feel almost dry. Don't get them too close to the fire, though— they can melt.

If you are unable to get a fire going after a cold-water cold-weather spill, get off the river as fast as you can: Head for the nearest warm environment. Ultimately, a victim of severe hypothermia can be kept alive by the age-old method whereby all party members strip off their clothes and huddle tightly around the hypothermic party member in whatever they can wrap around themselves for insulation. Body heat can save the life of a victim of hypothermia in extreme cases.

Whirlpools

Whirlpools occur where a powerful concentrated water flow opens into a suddenly widened riverbed. They also occur behind boulders, bridge abutments, and the like that block strong current flows. Most whirlpools on trout rivers aren't powerful enough to flip or suck under drift boats or rafts. There are some on powerful steelhead and white-water rivers that can, though, and canoes and smaller craft are much more at risk.

The rapid direction change of the current at the center of a whirlpool can have a similar effect to a hole. One side will be shoved under as the boat is abruptly swung around. Awareness and the use of human ballast are necessary, along with a continued attempt to avoid the heart of the whirlpool. Most whirlpools can be avoided, but beginning rowers sometimes find themselves in one due to a lack of attention or knowledge.

Almost every year someone drowns on the Missouri near where I live, a stretch of river that's big in volume but flat. Even though it's a relatively mellow flat-surfaced river, some of its whirlpools at higher water levels are very strong. When canoes are flipped, some people inadvertently swim into them. These whirlpools will jerk a drift boat around but will rarely flip one. I have been on more powerful rivers where the difference between the center of the whirlpool and its outer edges is several feet or more. I've experienced one that sucked the front end of a big 16-foot raft underwater! It's hard to row out of big whirlpools and worse swimming through them. Keep your eyes open and breathe when you can. You will come out before long, but it can seem a long time when you're under water!

The most turbulent situations occur where a heavy current runs by a boulder, cliff edge, or bridge abutment. The difference in current speed between the downstream main current flow and that of the water running upstream behind the impediment can be extreme. There can even be an altitude difference between the two. Pulling into a whirlpooling eddy right behind a boulder can upset a drift boat. Pulling back into the main current from right behind one can be even worse. Instead, pull in behind obstacles a little farther downstream, where the current difference isn't so extreme. The same goes for pulling out into the main current from behind a river-blocking feature: Drop downstream a bit before reentering a heavy current.

Effects of the Elements

Sun, wind, rain, snow, cold, and heat all influence the river in subtle to catastrophic ways. Wind, for example, is a rowing obstacle that you might not initially think of. Its effect on rafts and drift boats is great, though, because their surface area is large enough to be pushed by the wind. Drift boats are especially bad in this respect. The high sides and bottom curvature (rocker) that allow them to maneuver and handle rough water so well also means they blow like a leaf across the surface. This can be very disconcerting to a novice rower. A lazy straight stretch of river that's normally a no-brainer sees the boatman rowing like mad to keep his boat from getting slammed into the bank by a cross-wind. This can take more strength and endurance than running rapids, for the wind is often unrelenting. A downstream gale will shove you down the river faster than you want to go unless a rather brutal measure of back rowing is kept up every second (this is particularly rough on the palms of your hands!). An upstream blow can at times make downstream progress almost impossible. I have been in spots where even back rowing as hard as I could in the strongest current produced no downstream headway. We ended up taking the boat out of the river right there!

There are landscapes that concentrate wind and landscapes that block it. I know a spot on a canyon river where the wind tunnel effect is so pronounced that grass clumps on one bank will be divided with each half blown in opposite directions, just like parted hair! Some big-river valleys, like the Yellowstone, are known for their afternoon winds. Other, smaller rivers have a greater degree of wind block. Across the Rocky Mountain West, though, wind is a daily reality. Where I guide, wind is the biggest rowing obstacle. Water-related obstacles rate a distant second.

On the whole, cross-winds are the worst to row in. You often have to go down the river sideways, with your stern to the wind rather than against the current. You'll be rowing against a combination of the two. Fly fishers might not be having much fun at this point either! The chances of hooking each other with casts led astray by the wind go up with every gust!

Besides actually getting blown into banks, shallows, rocks, or what have you, beginners must be aware of oar dig, as discussed in Chapter 2. Don't allow the boat to get blown along at a high speed sideways and then dig your downwind oar. You'll find yourself getting unintentionally blown into some shallow areas, too, where the boat will start banging the streambed and your oars will have little grab or will get jammed into the bottom. What's important is to constantly maintain control and never let the boat get too much out of hand, especially if you are coming into a challenging bit of water.

On rivers that call for some trick maneuvering, wind can buffet you at inopportune moments, interfering at the last second with your set-up and subsequent rowing route. An extra level of attention and physical effort can be necessary.

You can learn to set up for wind gusts just as you would for other obstacles. You can actually see and hear wind gusts coming. Windblown water and waving grasses and trees let you know that a sudden blast is about to pound you. Wind direction is somewhat constant, so when you see a gust coming, position the boat to battle the wind as needed, swinging your stern into it, and lay on some heavy preliminary oar strokes. Look for the more sheltered, or lee, side of the river to float down. You might want to concentrate on wind-free areas by pulling over to anchor, wade-fishing them thoroughly. Rising trout don't like wind either. Wind-free slicks along protected banks might be the only places you'll find steadily rising fish. Ultimately, if you fish one or two favorite pieces of water most of the time whose rowing requirements aren't too challenging, you might want to buy a boat that has good wind-rowing properties above all else. We'll look at this more closely in Chapter 6.

Thunderstorms can present some extreme experiences. When I see those big, nasty clouds roll in too closely, I start looking for cover. There are plenty of willows where I guide, and these are great to take cover in. They're low, dense, and unlikely to be struck by lightning while at the same time blocking most wind, rain, and hail. Our thunderstorms don't last very long. It's their initial impact and potential wind speeds that are so menacing. I'll hang near some willows as a storm draws near, take cover when it hits, then get down the river a bit for the good fishing that often materializes when clouds and cool moist weather kick in. Should another thunderhead be rolling in, I'll be thinking of the next strategically placed willow grove and calculating how long I need to get there.

Lightning in mountain valleys seems to stay up pretty high, usually hitting somewhere on the upper half of the slopes. I don't worry about getting struck by lightning much on mountain rivers, though I do look for low, thick willows as cover. Prairie rivers are another matter. Lightning hits low and often. Winds are particularly fierce. The hail pummels. Here there might be no willows, only old and crumbling cottonwood groves. These are a lousy place to take cover because they're brittle and drop big limbs with regularity in big blows. Lightning strikes are distinct possibilities here, too. It's better to seek out whatever low dense brush you can to weather out a storm, perhaps following deer tracks a little way up a protected coulee.

Another thing you have to be careful of in wind storms is the anchoring of your boat. Enough wind will cause a boat to drag its anchor, especially if the anchor is on a short length of rope. A longer length of rope allows the anchor a better bite in the streambed. The rope angle when it's long produces less pressure on the anchor.

Here's an all too common thunderstorm scenario. A fishing party sees, smells, hears, and feels a big thunderhead rolling toward them. All agree it would be best to take cover. The party drops anchor near the bank, huddling in a storm-tight grotto. Feeling pretty secure, they might even light up a good cigar and settle in to watch the show. Powerful winds start hitting, dust flies, and the first rain and hail start pelting down. The boat is swinging on its rope. The wind increases, trees lean, thunder booms. Suddenly the boat starts towing the anchor out across the river—being anchored on too short a rope allowed the boat to drag it more easily. The deeper the water the boat blows out to, the less hold the anchor has. Eventually the boat reaches water that's deep enough that the anchor no longer touches the bottom. Off it goes downstream! Its owner scrambles to reach it in time, but it all happened so fast that he's last seen running downstream, splashing through the shallows downriver in hopes of retrieving his craft. Chances are it'll end up on the other side. He'll need to flag a boat ride to find it.

What I do when a big storm approaches is to pull my drift boat halfway up the bank so it won't blow around, release a long length of anchor rope, and wedge the anchor way up on dry land. I'll wrap the rope around a tree a couple of times for security, if a tree is available. You could as easily anchor your boat in shallow water with its rope fully extended. The problem here is that the boat can start swinging around on the long rope and is likely to repeatedly bang into stream-edge rocks, chipping the hull. One can also use a heavier anchor—thirty-five pounds should do it. Most drift boats in my area seem to favor thirty-pound anchors. If you get too heavy an anchor it will be a real chore pulling it in throughout the day and perhaps will be more work than it's worth.

If I have to park along a very steep rocky bank to sit out a storm, I'll usually stay with the boat the whole time, hail and all, to hold it and keep it from bashing itself against the rocks. This is one of those acts of love that wooden-boat owners are likely to display to preserve the finish of their handbuilt crafts.

Many rafts don't have an anchor system at all, and some owners don't even carry anchors. I've had to transport a few rafters who pulled their boat too lightly up the shore, only to have it blow away. Very cheap light rafts can even become airborne. I saw one blow across the wide Missouri once and get pinned up in some cliffs on the other side! The owners, who mistakenly left the raft alone on the bank to get their car, couldn't believe their plight! Always carry an anchor or a long tie-down rope of at least 25 feet. Trees don't always grow down to the edge of the water along some floodplain rivers. Raft owners need rope to make sure they can secure their boat in wind, especially if it's left alone.

Although wind on the whole is no friend of an oarsman, it does have a few benefits. It blows hoppers, terrestrial insects, and damselflies into the river, attracting larger trout. Light wind can ripple the water just enough to make trout less picky and spooky, because their vision becomes somewhat obscured. You can often get away with slightly larger flies and slightly heavier tippet in a light to medium wind chop. On those searing summer days a little breeze feels good, but only a little!

GLARE

Sunshine is another one of those less-tangible river obstacles that you might not consider unless you happen to be floating down a west-slope running river into a brilliant sunset! The sun can be blinding if it's in the wrong quarter. There's not much you can do about it besides the usual hat and Polaroids routine. On choppy rivers with a few rock gardens thrown in, the glare off waves and water droplets is too much to see through. I've found this to be the case on parts of Montana's Blackfoot River where it flows directly west.

If your eyes are particularly sensitive, you might want to consider the direction a river flows and the hours you fish it. Avoid east-flowing rivers at sunrise and west-flowing ones toward dusk. You might even choose to fish on overcast days, because these often produce better fishing anyway. Make sure you have a hat and sunglasses on hand to combat day-long glare, which is hard on the eyes.

When it comes to ease of viewing and especially spotting rising fish and trout *under* water, it's best to use a steep wooded bank as a viewing backdrop on your side of the river. Gaining ideal viewing positions can add up to more fish caught. In the float-fishing game, spotting fish is just as important as avoiding river obstacles.

Manmade Hazards

Although diversion dams top the list of hazardous manmade obstructions, there are a few others to be concerned with as well. Barbed-wire fences are stretched across some smaller rivers to keep cattle confined to their owners' properties. Some Fish and Game departments have designed "floater's gates" and installed them in place of barbed-wire fences. These curtainlike contraptions made of PVC pipe allow floaters to glide through them while psychologically detaining cattle, whose creative instincts for revolution and escape seem genetically limited!

Barbed-wire fences can be low and tight, requiring one or two party members to go out ahead of the boat and lift the fence strands before the boat tries to pass underneath it. Don't try to float up to a fence and lift it from the boat. If the fence can't be lifted high enough the boat can get pinned by the force of the current and punctured. People, too, are easily sliced by the barbs. Ultimately, it helps to keep some combination wire snips–needlenose pliers on board, plus a little length of wire or cord, especially if you know in advance that encountering

A nice trout hovers in an eddy picking off mayflies as the hatch wanes. Many trout can be spotted both rising and subsurface by the observant angler. It pays to hone trout-spotting skills, because you're likely to catch more fish when you know where they are.

fences is a possibility. If you have to cut a strand or two to get by, you can then repair the fence. Many landowners are already touchy enough about having people float through their property without having their cattle escape, too. These tools also come in handy for other repairs.

Irrigation canals pose potential problems on some rivers. They can head off a river and appear to be just another side channel. After getting down one a little way, you'll probably run into a small dam or gate. Now, having realized your dilemma, you have to pull your boat back upstream to the main channel again, which isn't always an easy task. Many western hay meadows are flood-irrigated from these canals, which breed hordes of blood-sucking mosquitoes. I've heard a few tales of woe about dragging boats back up out of irrigation canals while swatting madly and being devoured by mosquitoes. Naturally, such adventures in floating are most likely to happen on balmy summer days, when the chosen attire is shorts and wading sandals!

Bridge pilings and low bridges are common hazards, too. Some are tight squeezes in strong currents and call for controlled rowing. High water makes some low bridges unpassable. This makes their discovery by an unsuspecting party rather critical, necessitating a tedious to difficult portage. On some rivers there are old pilings that are just barely submerged and capable of ripping rafts. Old car bodies once used to brace eroding banks, fence posts, and other farm debris are common in riverbeds and feature sharp boat-piercing metal. Sunken trees and waterlogged limbs might also have to be watched for and rowed around.

Between the use of modern floaters' maps, books, and advice from local Fish and Game departments and fishing shops, float fishers should be able to learn of most river hazards in advance. They should be otherwise alert and able to recognize different dangers and know how to row or portage around them. Once safety, knowledge, and rowing skills are ingrained, the fishing potential gets better and better.

4

FLOAT-FISHING STRATEGIES: IMPROVING YOUR CATCH RATE

A row boat is an effective fishing tool only when the boatman understands trout behavior and rows for the fisherman's advantage. Just being in a boat doesn't guarantee better fishing. Indeed, it can be a detriment if it's not properly controlled, if the boat whisks by hot spots that should be slowed or stopped for. Let's examine several facets of float-fishing with a goal of improving your catch rate.

Thinking Like a Trout

Being a successful trout fisher, a really successful one, hinges on understanding trout behavior—their needs, moods, feeding habits, fears, and seasonal peculiarities. From a float-fishing perspective, knowing where trout hold in a river is the highest priority. Being able to cast well and accurately *and* being able to control line drag once the fly is on the water rates a close second. Knowing what local trout are eating is important, but even generalized patterns will catch fish if casts and line control are good. It's easier to find out what the current hatches are than it is to learn to cast and fish well. Finally, there can be some equipment that must be had at times to routinely catch fish. For instance, late-spring conditions can produce rising muddy waters where only a well-sunk stonefly nymph might bring regular success. If you don't have the weighted nymphs and weighting system to get line, leader, and fly near the bottom, it could cut your catch rate.

Trout have few immediate needs in life: eat, survive, spawn. Although they need moving water and its conveyance of food, trout don't want too much of a good thing. They hold in places where moderated currents prevail, a good food supply is delivered, and safety is close at hand. Off to the sides of the main current is where most fish will be, or under them along the bottom.

The rower's mind is alert to the trout's needs. He positions anglers where they can most effectively fish for trout—within casting range and where the best line control can be exerted so that drag is minimized. He must also position the boat so it's least likely to be seen by the fish. It's an added advantage if the boat can be rowed in place or anchored in this optimal position as long as necessary to achieve success. In other cases, when no particular hot spots are on hand, just slowing the boat down and keeping it a constant distance from the target bank or water will be the top rowing priority. There will be places where it's best to pull over and wade-fish for optimal results.

Perhaps the best way to look at some of the trout's favorite hangouts is to take a hypothetical stretch of river and analyze various water types one at a time. Our prototype river will be medium large. This will allow us to explore most situations found on western trout rivers. Our conclusions might also be applied to smallmouth bass and other species. Stream character, fish behavior, and hatches vary from river to river, though, even in the same geographic area and with the same species of fish. Serious rowing anglers keep their minds open and attentive to such idiosyncrasies. Float-fishing for trout can be a series of problem-solving experiences, and the biggest problem, navigation aside, is not catching fish!

Before starting down the river, let's consider a few things. Fish could be on either side of the river almost anywhere along our route. The crew will naturally want to choose the side with the best concentrations of fish and the most well-defined trout holding water. On a small river, each caster could take a side. On big rivers, one side or the other should be chosen. And although the most obvious and well-defined trout spots can be easy enough to figure out, the more subtle holding waters will be of great interest, too. There might already be anglers at many of the obvious places. Understanding the second-best choices, therefore, can be important, and on many occasions it's those spots that will make a day. There are many small hot spots in a river that may hold only a fish or two. Added up over the course of a day's fishing, this can tally a good percentage of the catch.

POSITION I

Our trip finds us floating down the long belly of a straight stretch of river (refer to the illustration on page 95), heading toward the tailout. Commonly, one side will be a little bit steeper, deeper, and swifter than the other (usually this is the outside bank leading down from the previous bend in the river). This is our A side. The opposite side will be a little shallower and slower-paced.

The A side is the deeper of the two, and chances are there might be an undercut bank, fallen chunks of eroded turf, and perhaps a big rock or log or two all creating eddying fish hangouts. The trout along this side are apt to be concentrated closer to the bank, thus offering anglers a more desirable-looking target area to cast to. Grass-bordered banks are another good possibility. Fish can be used to seeing hoppers, crickets, beetles, ants, and other land-based insects become part of their diet. Such fish can be easier to fool with a broader array of patterns.

There will be a tendency for both anglers to want to cast to the most likely looking spots all through the day. The bow angler will hit such hot spots first. The stern angler will hit it immediately afterward. Other water might be ignored. Unless the bow fisherman is a bad caster and really not covering these spots well the first time, the stern rod would be better off covering a different drift lane than the first rod did. And unless one hot fly pattern has already proven to be the best, floating anglers might do better trying varying fly types.

For instance, the bow rod could run a dry fly a few feet out from the bank, targeting subtle eddy lines and pockets, while the stern angler drops a streamer, nymph, or contrasting dry fly closer in. In this way two feed lanes are covered rather than one, and a variety of flies are experimented with until the best-producing ones are found. These hot patterns are likely to change with time and in different water types. In this way, too, the bow rod doesn't hit the close-in water at all, thus leaving the stern angler some unfished, unspooked trout.

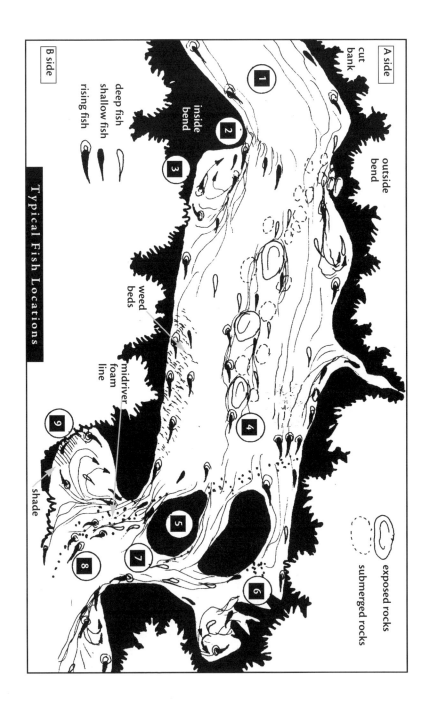

Typical Fish Locations

A side

cut bank

outside bend

B side

inside bend

deep fish
shallow fish
rising fish

weed beds

midriver foam line

shade

exposed rocks
submerged rocks

The center of the river undoubtedly holds some fish, but it's such a flat, monotonous, and possibly deep glide of water that few will choose to fish it. A deep-swimming well-sunk streamer on a full sinking line would be a possibility, but it's a possibility most will ignore. During a profuse hatch trout could be rising here and there out in the middle, especially if a big foam line wanders downstream. In this case the fish are giving themselves away and make good targets. On the whole, though, most floaters will choose one side or the other in such a stretch.

Along the B side of the river at position 1 is a slower-paced, shallow sheet of water that can look very uniform, boring, and unproductive. However, there can be quite a few trout (and whitefish) scattered along here. Some nice fish will hold surprisingly close to the shore in just inches of water because few anglers bother them and chase them out. Because trout here are scattered and sparse, most floaters choose the A side. But when a good hatch is on, a surprising number of trout can materialize along this slower side, giving excellent match-the-hatch fishing. In that case it can be better to pull over and wade-fish to those steady risers. The uniform flows make presentations easy, but the clear water allows fish to look over your fly, and they *can* be picky.

It's always a good idea to stop and concentrate on a good hatch. You never know when the wind might come up in the west—these could be the last rising fish you see for the day! On the other hand, a perfect day might show you so many rising fish and therefore slow your progress down so much that you'll have to navigate your way off the river in the dark if you don't pay attention to your time and mileage schedule.

If no hatch is on along the B side, it's most effectively fished by using long drifts of a dry fly (with each angler's fly covering different feed lanes), by dry-fly–nymph-dropper combinations, or by streamer fishing. Streamers should be dropped up close to the bank and fished all the way back to the boat, for trout can be widely scattered. This covers a lot of water, and you can gaze around at the scenery, something that many serious anglers seem to forget to do!

As we proceed downriver from position 1 to position 2, we enter what's known as the tail of the pool, or tailout. The streambed often widens here temporarily and becomes shallow. Trout are fond of rising here during good hatches due to the gradually upsloping bottom and slowing currents. They can be spread all the way across the river. When not rising, they'll seem nonexistent or widely scattered. During a profuse hatch this can be a prime area to anchor and wade. You could drop one fisherman off on one side of the river, row across, anchor on the other side, and fish there, too. Anglers could then work their way up both sides or to wherever fish are sighted. Many tailouts allow an easy row across the river without sweeping the boat on downstream. Others have swifter centers and take more power to cross.

Position 2

As we approach position 2 the river makes a sharp curve, eroding one side and often leaving a gravel beach on the other. This is a classic pool-riffle-pool sequence on a big-river scale. It can be a real hot spot with fish concentrated behind the drop-off on the inside bend (the B side). You can float-fish it, making a point to not row over the best trout water, then pull over below and walk back up to wade-fish.

There can be a variety of fish-holding spots here. Along bank A are usually some swift-water pockets that hold fish. From a boat these are often one-shot deals, because the current can be whisking you along at a pretty good rate, even if you are back rowing like mad. It's good attractor-pattern, nymph, and streamer water, and big fish might be found. You can float-fish this outside bend, then cross over, anchor, and wade-fish the riffle drop-off on the inside bend. You could also drop one angler off along that steeper outside bend to walk-fish his way back up, covering those enticing pockets thoroughly.

Downstream in the center is a drop-off, sometimes rock- and boulder-studded, which is capable of housing many trout. This is a deep-nymphing prospect. If you can get your nymphs (or streamers) to the bottom and fish it systematically while wade-fishing, excellent results could be had. You could float-fish it, too, with heavy nymphs, weighted leaders, and strike indicators, but that is usually a decided second choice for most floaters. It's better to pull over and wade-fish the center, time allowing. In these days of heavier fishing pressure, though, all alternatives are explored and perfected, including midriver nymphing from the boat.

Shallow riffle corners on the inside bends of big rivers are great places to find rising trout and to cover the water with nymphs and streamers. Rising trout will hold in the very shallow water, too, just inches from the gravelly banks. Stopping to look and wade-fish in such locations can increase your day's catch.

Closer to the B bank, the drop-off becomes shallow. It's easier to cover and can hold concentrations of trout, especially on big tailwater rivers. A dry-fly–nymph-dropper combination is a good starting set-up. During a hatch many rising fish might be found, though they can be tougher to spot in the choppy waves. Some will move surprisingly close to the bank in ultrashallow water, including the largest rising fish to be found. Indicator nymphing is always a good bet here, and streamers produce, too.

When a boat floats by such drop-offs, expectations are high. The rower should slow down as much as possible as the anglers cover different feed lanes. There can also be a distinct eddy line or two that should be targeted. Doubles are possible in this type of water. It's an area to concentrate on between hatches if the mood to wade-fish strikes you, and a great place to find rising fish as well when the hatches come.

Position 3

Just behind the actual drop-off on the B side is a distinct eddy known to some as the eye of the pool. In some cases the current just moderates, with no back-swirling eddy being formed. Either way, it's a favorite spot for trout to hold in. Food is abundant, and they can fin easily in the slower water. The sanctuary of midriver is but a few wiggles away. Trout can be scattered across this eddy zone, from the inches-deep bank out to what's often a distinct but broadening eddy line. On smaller water there might just be one or two fish. It can be roughly covered from the boat, but the boat's motion and the eddying currents make it hard to get a long drift of the fly. The line can start dragging before some trout will choose to take. (Gung ho wilderness trout can be eager enough to jump on it when it first lands.) Stopping to wade-fish the eye is best, after first scouting it for the noses of rising fish.

Out across midstream near position 3 is the belly of the pool. It's usually deep, rock-studded, and fish-holding. On gravel-bottom rivers there are drop-offs and depressions that also will contain trout. It's deep nymph and streamer territory, except on small shallow rivers where fish might take surface flies without having to come up through too much water. There can be plenty of fish spread over a large area, including schools of whitefish and many trout. Time allowing, this, too, could be wade-fished most effectively.

Along the deeper A side of position 3 is often a steeper eroded bank. It can be rock-studded and have some high-water log debris left there. Bank pockets and riffle lines are numerous. It's the kind of float-fishing water that has great eye appeal and fish, too, though there are usually more overall trout back on the B side in positions 2 to 3. Nonetheless, it's a fish producer.

Trout will rise here during a hatch and take attractor patterns if the mood hits. It's excellent nymph water most any time. Trout are used to grabbing naturals that wash out of the fast water upstream. A dry-fly–nymph-dropper rig is a good choice, too, as are indicator nymphs and streamers. Many feeding trout prefer to sit upstream of rocks along these types of banks and in the river's center, rather than behind them. This is something to remember when fishing broken pocket water.

The boatman should do his best to slow the boat down to a near standstill while the anglers cover different feed lanes and pockets, as many as possible. It's not usually a good place to anchor a boat. The swift current can actually pull the stern end of the boat

Rock-studded and riprap banks provide plenty of holding pockets for trout. Some will be seen rising and just subsurface, others will merely be anticipated. The boat's position relative to a targeted eddy is very important when trying to get a perfect drift.

under water when it is anchored in too heavy a flow. The boat can also swing wildly from side to side on the anchor rope and possibly flip. In other cases, the anchor won't hold and will be dragged downstream. Sometimes the anchor will snag among rocks and prove to be irretrievable. It will have to be cut loose. I always consider bottom structure and current speed before dropping my anchor.

A good way to fish the pocket water along the fast-water bank is to pull the boat over near the tailout after float-fishing it and let one angler systematically walk-fish his way back up. Few people do this, and it can be quite productive. The fish *are* there!

POSITION 4

As the river slows and widens, it fans out into the tail of the pool much as in position 1. In this case its character differs, eventually splitting into an island system.

On spring-rich and tailwater rivers, the B side here will grow profuse weed beds and support many trout. Expansive flats can be found, where during a hatch many steady-rising fish will be giving their positions away. This is great water to stop and wade. Big fish can hold in extreme shallows, too. Look for big noses and pulsing wakes!

Hunt your quarry during a hatch rather than fishing blind.

Midriver could be shallow enough to still show rising trout. It could also just deepen into a zone of little interest. Some big trout can hang here, though, and fall victim to wideswept streamers fished deep.

The A bank could continue to have rock pockets, though with a mellower flow, or it, too, could widen out into a tailout flats. Either way, it's likely to hold fish and be a fun area to cover. It's a good place to be during a hatch and also fishes well blind because there's often enough definition (for instance, ripple lines, pockets) to make targeting imagined fish practical.

This is easy water to row. Fish that are seen can be picked off from the boat. The rower should be able to hold the boat in place in the current or anchor within ideal casting range of specific targets. Let your anchor down slowly, though. It can scare fish when it thuds the bottom and scrapes across the gravel before holding. The streambed of a tailout is generally formed of finer gravel and cobblestones that settle out of the current after tumbling through the faster water drop-off upstream in high water. It's normally a good anchoring and wading area that will feature rising trout.

POSITION 5

Island systems frequently result from erosion as rivers cut corners and carve new channels. The usual scenario sees islands loom into view at the tailout of one run and form part of the drop-off that heads the next one. Series of gravel bars, some connecting island to island, can be found. Their riffles, eddy lines, streambed depressions, and drop-offs all hold the promise of trout.

Just upstream of most islands is a tailout. The river becomes shallow as it approaches the head of the island (the upstream end). Trout like to hold here. This is most interesting during a hatch, when many fish seemingly materialize out of thin air (or water).

There can be gravel bars leading from bank to island and island to island. Sometimes they can be waded across, though on big rivers perhaps not. In either case, there's likely to be gravel bar drop-offs and depressions that can be real hot spots, good places to nymph blind or to spot rising fish during a hatch.

The tailouts of big rivers can widen, forming extensive shallow flats that are suitable for wading. Some have midriver gravel bars, as in the photograph, or lead into island systems. Both variations can show good numbers of rising fish during a hatch.

Next come the ripple lines that peel off the heads of islands and the slower fish-holding water just downstream of them. These can be much like the situation back at position 2, side B, but on a smaller, gentler scale. They can be excellent dry-fly riffles. Nymphs, two-fly rigs, and streamers all work well here.

At the ends of islands are converging currents, drop-offs, and eddies. These can be great indicator-nymphing locations between hatches, with trout ganged up in this ideal holding water. During a hatch some rising fish will push forward closer to the drop-off. Others might fall back or follow slow-coursing foam lanes, rising where food concentrates most.

It's always a good idea to stop and look for rising trout before blindly wading in to cast. Check the shallow water nearest the island banks first and scan out from there. During a good hatch you can pinpoint all the possible targets, then proceed to fish for them in an order that's least likely to scare subsequent risers off. Several good trout might be landed from the same casting position. Islands are always favorite places to stop and wade-fish.

Thinking about how to maximize your opportunities can lead to more fish caught. For instance, if you wade-fish the ripple line peeling off the head of a small island first, the silt you kick up could put down the trout that were rising in the drop-off at the tail. It would be better to look over the whole situation, start fishing the tail, then work your way back up to the head. You'll even want to watch where you pull in your boat to land, making sure you don't row over rising fish or the most likely trout-holding water.

On larger rivers, trout show a fondness for smaller side channels. They often concentrate there, sometimes in surprising numbers. It seems as if they prefer the confinement of a small channel over the universe of wide-open water. If no rising fish are found, get nymphs down near the bottom, or sweep a streamer. You can often fish a streamer first and pull out the most aggressive fish, wait a couple minutes, then go back through with an indicator nymph and pick off more. A couple switches in nymph patterns might yield additional fish. On freestone rivers, medium to large nymphs can produce best. On tailwaters and spring-fed rivers, small nymphs are likely to be better

Island systems provide excellent trout habitat. These floaters are hitting the converging currents at the end of an island, where waters deepen and many trout may hold.

choices. Fishing two varying nymphs at a time is a good idea, too. Different sizes, colors, and patterns can be experimented with.

POSITION 6

Position 6 finds us at a deeply eroded bank littered with flood debris and overhanging logs. Little foam lanes trickle across the dark slow pool, leading down from the ripple drop-off back up the side channel. Such spots are common enough and most always house some trout. If the hillside behind is steep and light reflection is blocked, trout here can often be spotted cruising just beneath the surface, as trout are wont to do. Others will stay under the cover of the bank, showing themselves but occasionally. Still others might stay deep, feeding on what the side channel brings in. I know of many locations like this.

Some trout here can be spotted, stalked, and caught from a rowed or anchored boat. Rowing the boat to a standstill should be no problem in water like this. It's always fun and educational to stalk visible trout; there's something to learn about trout behavior in every encounter. If no fish are in evidence, a Woolly Bugger here is a good choice. You could also systematically cover the water with a nymph or large dry like a hopper or Humpy. A big twitched dry can draw some fish to the surface from afar.

POSITION 7

Below the island system, side channels reconverge. Gravel bar drop-offs can be extensive, and most can hold trout. During a hatch you might find risers concentrated in subtle eddies behind minichannels that pour over such bars. Fish can also stack up in the upper part of the regrouped channel. The bottom configuration gives them shelter from the current while dumping in plenty of food. This is another spot that's best fished by pulling over and nymphing systematically. Some rising fish can be found during hatches, but more might be caught deep.

When floating, you can hold the boat just behind riffle drop-offs with surprising ease. As the water drops over a gravel bar into a trough, it creates a mini hole, one that's not visible yet helps to hold the boat in place there. A rower can move back and forth across such drop-offs, letting anglers cover the water before rowing over it. You can row across a river behind a gravel bar in this fashion with little effort. You could anchor, too, and jump out to wade-fish if it's shallow enough, though some less-agile anglers might have a hard time getting back up into the boat. Watch for loose gravel at the drop-off edge, or you could slide and sink into much deeper water and be carried off downstream.

POSITION 8

Here we see a slow deep channel and rather featureless water accented with a wandering midriver foam line. Watch these closely during and after a hatch or spinner fall. Trout can gather and cruise there, rising to the food that concentrates in such foam. The current can be slow enough that trout can hold there all day. Sometimes you just see rings of rising fish. Other times, in more ideal viewing conditions, you can see the fish themselves finning just below the surface and looking to it for a meal.

POSITION 9

The point on side B at position 9 is similar to that back at positions 2 and 3, but the current is slower and the surface smoother.

Some bits of foam and weed might be found circulating in the eddy here, and it's a good place to find a few rising fish during and after a hatch. Some might push up into and fan out along the edge of the eddy line. Others will cruise the big quiet eddy or hold near the bank edge.

This bank is deep and tree-bordered. The resulting shade is an attraction to fish. It gives them cover from the sun and predatory birds (while also giving these same birds a place to perch!), plus an added source of food in the form of terrestrial insects. In very hot weather the shade might even indicate the few places you'll find actively feeding fish. I like to row a boat to a standstill in such spots and look hard for cruising trout. Some might ease in and out of view beneath the foliage and require exacting casts. This can be one of those cases where sitting and watching for a while can be more productive than immediately slapping a fly down. On the other hand, I recall casting damselfly dry flies down in spots like this and seeing trout come zooming over to pounce on them. Those slow shady spots are always worth an extra minute or two of inspection time, regardless of the outcome. A slow-swimming Woolly Bugger, twitched dry, or a twist-retrieved nymph might pull out a fish.

Although it would be impossible to mention every river and trout-holding configuration, this short trip certainly covers many of them. A good hatch makes it easier to explore a new reach of river, for the fish then give their positions away. Even between hatches some fish will rise. Others can be seen under the water by those who constantly look for them. Polaroid sunglasses and a backdrop that blocks glare from the sky help immensely. And of course there are big trout that rarely rise and can't be seen. Successful float fishers will be imagining where the best trout water should be while keeping their eyes peeled for surface and subsurface trout throughout the day.

Rowing a Casting Platform

An oarsman can help anglers in several ways. He's an integral part of the fishing and not a detached onlooker. It's a teamwork effort that works best if all in the party are on top of their game. The boat is nothing more than a rowed platform from which to cast. Whether it's near the bank, upstream, outside, or downstream of its quarry, its position and motion should be deliberately chosen to produce the desired results.

The rower's first priority (besides safety) is to slow the boat down by using a steady back-rowing pace. This gives anglers time to assess the water (on both sides and in the center of the river), to look for risers and subsurface trout, and to cover the river as thoroughly as possible.

Equally important is keeping the craft a steady distance from the bank or target water as much as possible so that fly casters can work with a uniform length of line. You shouldn't be so close as to scare fish off or so far as to make casting time-consuming, difficult, or impossible. Thirty-five to 50 feet away would be a good generic working distance. On shallow, ripply, and rough-surfaced rivers you can get a little closer to the fish without them seeing you. On deeper, slow, slick-surfaced rivers, you'll need to stay a little farther away.

There will be times, of course, when the rower can't keep a specific distance from a bank and will have to get closer to it. This is usually due either to a narrow channel or because of executing a hazard maneuver. Sometimes the current or wind will inadvertently push you closer into a bank than you meant to go (as will inattention to your duties). What anglers can do in these cases, besides the obvious choice of shortening their lines, is to cast farther downstream from the boat using the same length of line. The boat can be pushed right up against the bank and they can still continue to fish effectively. They'll have to be on guard to avoid tangling lines, but a more downstream, rather than across-stream, presentation will certainly fool a high percentage of fish while allowing casters to go on using the same length of line.

If the rower has to pull farther away from the target water to miss a hazard, the casters can either lengthen line or fish around the hazard. You don't want to lengthen your fly line to an extreme degree, because it then becomes more and more likely that you might hook someone in the boat on a bad cast. You could also just let your fly drag out from the bank and appreciate the panoramic scenery for a moment. It's surprising how many fish are caught when a fly is allowed to skitter across deeper water!

As the boatman back rows his way downstream, his eyes and

mind constantly scan the river, summing up the most likely trout water. He might ferry back and forth across-stream numerous times, choosing trout zones and putting anglers within casting range of the most likely ones. More maneuvering will be done to gain the best fishing positions than is done to avoid hazards. Back-rowing intensity will vary, too: an easy pace for mediocre stretches, a vigorous yet quiet pace for extra-productive-looking spots (you don't want to scare fish with splashy oar strokes or boat noise). You might row to a standstill, anchor, or disembark to wade-fish a prime location, or you might go a little more with the flow to deep-nymph a long undercut bank. (Vigorous back rowing won't allow a nymph to sink deeply and get a long drift.) Each water type can call for a slightly different approach, both in boat speed and position.

The position of a boat in relation to a fish or hot spot can be important to success. There are any number of positions you could be in that are 40 feet from your target—upstream, directly across, downstream, to the inside, or to the outside. But only one of them might allow *the* perfect drift of your fly over the fish without undue drag— just being within casting range isn't always enough.

For this reason the oarsman must also be considering things from the fly caster's point of view, something that many novice rowers initially fail to comprehend. When I guide, I'm thinking largely of the fly line and its optimal angle and placement in relation to a trout. I know there's a certain distance that can be managed by each caster, and one best angle of approach. Remember that the boat is usually out toward midriver in swifter water, whereas the fish is in closer to the bank in slower currents. There can be eddies and current variances in between, too. I often tell my guests that I'm going to ease slowly into the perfect position and then tell them when to cast. Human nature leads some to cast a little early, when the fish really isn't in perfect range yet. It's eagerness that steers them. The fly usually starts dragging just as it comes up to the trout's position. If they had waited until I floated 5 feet closer, the perfect drift could have been achieved. This kind of subtlety is very important when casting to larger, spookier rising fish.

Casting from a boat is in some ways the opposite of wade-fishing a stream. The latter sees most casts made up- and across-stream.

Anglers often wade in slower water near the bank and cast up into swift water. Float fishers are generally doing things the other way around. They're in swift water casting to slow water. What works best from the boat is to cast somewhat downstream at close to a 45-degree angle. The line must land with some slack built into it, though. It then straightens as it approaches its target. I might stop back rowing for a few seconds or even row forward just a bit to help extend the drift of a dry fly I think is going to pass perfectly over a trout's position. (Vigorous back rowing naturally tends to straighten the leader and causes drag at a faster rate.) After the fly passes beyond the trout's position, I might then back row like mad, possibly returning upstream a bit to regain the ideal casting angle. What we're seeing here is that the ideal boat position in relation to a fish is most often just upstream of it.

Once you get even with or just downstream of a trout or pocket, that swifter current near the boat makes it harder and harder to get a long drag-free drift. There are ways to do it, but it's easier and better to get a longer drift from a slightly upstream angle. This goes against the grain of some small-stream-bred anglers' habits.

Let's briefly consider the merits, subtleties, and difficulties of casting to a fish from different boat positions (see the illustration on page 110). These could be while the boat is being rowed or anchored.

POSITION 1

Once in a while a rising fish will be spotted in such a position that the only probable angle for a good drift will be from directly upstream. I find this most along steeper rocky banks where little channels between boulders and swirling eddies make presentations from other angles difficult at best. The fish is spotted, the situation is assessed, and the boat is pulled in parallel to the bank at a workable casting distance.

You could drop the anchor here, but be careful about stirring up bottom silt with it, which could put the fish down. I often choose to row using the crawl stroke. The sweeping oar is nearest the bank. Sometimes you can just lay the bankside oar across some rocks and half-wedge it there while making easy back strokes with the midriver oar.

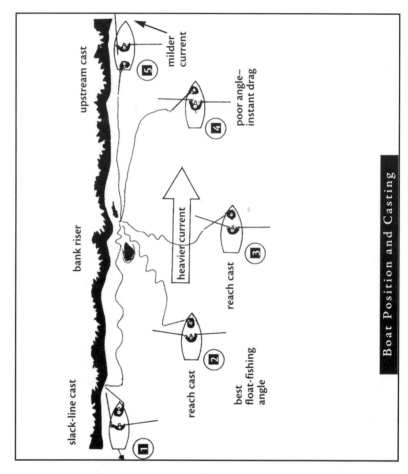

The caster needs to use an extreme slack-line cast and perhaps feed additional line out to get the fly over the trout. If it doesn't take on the first couple drifts the fish could easily spook, because you now have to retrieve leader and fly back upstream by the trout before making another cast. A little extra time and stealth between casts so as not to alert the fish can win the day. An extra long light tippet helps, too. I have guests who catch plenty of trout this way. Obviously, only one angler can fish in this situation.

Position 2

The boat in position 2 is at the best overall angle for most float-fishing presentations. A slightly down and across presentation using a slack-line reach cast allows long drag-free drifts, even across eddy lines. It also shows trout the fly before the leader, which helps fool pickier fish. It's an easy cast to do—every float fisher needs to master it (see page 117).

From position 2 to position 3 will be your best bet generally. The boatman may be able to row the boat to a standstill here. I'll often anchor at position 2 to work a trout or school of rising fish more thoroughly. You have to slow your boat down and plan to drop anchor before you get to the actual position, because the boat will end up downstream of the anchor itself and may drag it a bit before it takes hold. Trout can spook when an anchor hits the bottom and drags. They'll usually resume rising in a minute or two, though, so wait them out. The denser the hatch, the sooner they'll resume rising. You can wait them out if you spook them with casts, too. Sometimes It's best to pause a while between each presentation to keep from frightening the fish.

Position 3

When you reach the point where you're even with your fish, long dead-drift presentations start becoming more difficult to achieve. The act of casting directly across the main current and eddy lines now has a more immediate effect on your fly line. Drag sets in quicker than it did from the slightly upstream position.

Here again, a slack-line reach cast is best. It can be a little more extreme, with the rod reached upstream as far as you can easily manage. This allows you to show your fly to the fish before the leader and achieves the longest possible drag-free presentations. If you were to cast a straight line to the fish, as many anglers habitually do, drag would set in almost immediately. A few overenthusiastic trout will take a dragging fly, but many more will engulf a well-presented fly on a reach cast. An immediate mend might be necessary, too.

Position 4

Once you are downstream of the fish it becomes difficult to get much of a drag-free drift. The main current quickly grabs your fly

Casting down and across-stream with a reach cast at about a 45-degree angle works best in most float-fishing, because the boat is out in faster water and moving downstream while the fish are holding in slower water, often near the banks. This approach affords the longest drag-free dry-fly drifts but goes against the up-and-across custom most wade fishers are used to.

line no matter how it's cast and begins dragging it away. A skilled caster might use a tuck cast with some extra slack built in and buy a little time, but this is decidedly a tough angle for dry-fly work from a drift boat unless it is in a giant eddy or very slow stretch or river. When fishing streamers, however, many trout seem to like the down and across angle in which the wet fly swims. Perhaps it better imitates a baitfish in trouble. In any case, many fish are caught with Woolly Buggers and similar streamers fished from various angles from the banks.

Anglers usually find themselves fishing from position 4 only when the rower can't keep them in the positions 2 or 3 due to current speed. It might be worth trying that last shot back upstream to a rising fish or hot spot! When just fishing the water with no rising fish in sight, anglers will want to maintain a slightly down and across angle of their fly lines for the longest drag-free drifts.

POSITION 5

Should that trout still be rising after the boat has drifted by it, it's a good idea to pull over along the bank and try it from below. You can anchor, row to a standstill, or let an angler out on the bank. This will be a classic up-and-over casting approach, familiar to every wade and bank fisher. Some guides will jump out and walk the boat upstream into casting range, either bow or stern first, depending on which angler's turn it is to have a go at the fish. Taking turns casting in one-fish situations is the name of the game. This avoids fly-line tangles and is less likely to spook fish. If a number of trout are seen rising in a row tight to a productive bank, some floaters will opt to land below them all, walk the bank back upstream, and work one fish at a time. I generally prefer to try them first from the boat using the down and across reach cast from position 2. Some trout seem less wary when approached from this direction. If anglers can't make good, controlled reach casts, then fishing from below is a good backup option.

Every river encounter is a little different, but all need to be assessed in order to find and capitalize on the best angle of presentation for the angler. It's the rower's job to put and keep the boat in that position as long as necessary or possible. A quick conference between rower and casters might be in order to decide what that position is, but no time should be wasted in planning the course of action. When doing a straightforward "float by," anglers will want to recognize that there is a premium angle and moment to drop that fly in a trout's feed lane. Skilled casters will be able to stretch the limits of that angle to a greater degree.

As you row into position, avoid kicking up waves with the boat and oars. This can put fish down in calmer waters. Some anglers use too much body english when casting. This rocks a drift boat from side to side, putting out waves that have been known to scare a few flat-water trout. Also avoid dropping things in the boat or making loud clunking sounds, which transmit from boat hull to water.

One can only get so close to a trout before it sees the boat and flees. The flatter and deeper the water, the easier trout can spot you. Beginning fly fishers may have a difficult time casting far enough with the proper accuracy and control to fool rising fish on some calm rivers. They would do better on swifter, choppier rivers, where the trout's vision is obscured by waves, which means you can approach them more closely. Such trout tend to be "grabbier," too.

The rower can also help out once a trout takes a fly. Trout holding near a bank often race for midstream when hooked, which is right at the boat. Trout will run toward the boat, by it, or even under it, then continue on toward midriver. This can make it difficult for an angler to reel up line fast enough to keep the fish under tension. I'll often start back rowing away from the bank when a fish takes, anticipating this likely scenario. This can help an angler keep a tight line on his trout as it runs for midstream. If the fish just wallows near the bank or runs in some different direction, I'll adjust my rowing to the situation. Some fish will need to be followed downstream or led away from tangling cover. The boat can play a strategic role in the landing of a fine specimen. The rower or other angler can also do the netting, which can help increase the odds of success. Some anglers prefer fighting their trout from the bank, in which case the rower can drop them at the bank, making sure the boat's out of the angler's way.

All these aspects of float-fishing will come into play at some time in future journeys. Anticipating the possibilities goes toward improving your fishing day.

5

FLY FISHING FROM A BOAT: STRATEGIES FOR SAFE AND CONTROLLED CASTING

*T*here are some special aspects of fly fishing from a boat that need to be considered. Because the casters and rower are in close proximity, safety in casting becomes a major concern. So does avoiding tangles.

Because anglers in a boat often cast simultaneously, they need to keep their flies on parallel flight paths. Whenever they deviate from this general rule, tangles on the backcast or forward cast are bound to happen. Taking turns casting helps, too. It's easier for the angler in the back of the boat to watch the bow angler and cast when he's finished. A little verbal communication about your casting intentions helps, too, especially if you're about to cast out of parallel. An example would be making a last upstream cast to a rising fish the boat has drifted by. Parallel casts at a slight downstream angle (up to 45 degrees) is the name of the game.

Distance casting, casting in high winds, and the fishing of extra-heavy nymphs and streamers call for added attention, for the chances of hooking a boatmate are higher in these conditions. Make sure there is no slack line on the water when you begin your backcast. Strip your fly line in and start your backcast on a tight line with your rod tip held low near the water. Make your backcasts extrahigh to clear the boat's crew. Watch some of your backcasts to make sure their flight paths stay high. A sudden scream usually indicates a low backcast and the subsequent low and dangerous forward cast!

The fisherman in the back of the boat will have to be aware of the

This brown took the hopper end of a two-fly rig. Note the Beadhead Pheasant Tail Nymph on the angler's hand. Two-fly rigs allow added coverage of the water when prospecting for trout. This particular fly combination is good for late summer.

rower's oar strokes. When the boatman reaches back with the oars to begin his next stroke, they often cross the path of the stern angler's drifting fly line. The stern angler needs to lift his fly rod a bit to allow the oar to pass under his fly line, otherwise frequent tangles between line and oar will ensue. He must do this consistently to keep from ruining the rower's cadence, positioning, and peace of mind! The rower should not be interrupted by the stern angler's fly line, especially in critical maneuvering moments.

When safe and controlled casting has been mastered, attention and fishing time can be spent covering and exploring the water with a fly. (It's amazing how many hours of a fishing day can be spent untangling lines when the casters aren't in sync!) Visible rising fish aside, anglers will want to cover eligible-looking water as systematically as possible. The rower does his part by assessing the water, his positioning, and by slowing the craft down so that anglers can pick up their fly at the end of its drift, make a false cast or two, and drop the fly back out about where the last drift ended.

Covering the water is best achieved when anglers run their flies down different feed lanes. The first rod, in the front of the boat, can run his a little way out of the bank. The stern rod can fish closer in. In this way a broader zone of the river is covered and both casters have an equal chance of success. There are water types (such as a deep under-cut bank) where the likely trout-holding positions are so confined that both anglers will want to run their flies over the same lanes and pockets. Other times, though, there are eddies, pockets, and ripple lines against, near, and peeling out from the bank. These present the two anglers with a broader zone of potential fish water that's best covered by fishing different lanes.

Still better coverage can be had by fishing two fly rigs. Flies can be spaced 1–3 feet apart, offering fish both a dry and a nymph, while widening the zone covered by both anglers a little farther. Having the stern rod sweep a streamer (or two) covers even more trouty terrain. Should one fly pattern prove to be the best producer, you could fish it alone or tie two on.

Special Casting Techniques

There are just a few casting adaptations that make fishing from a boat more productive. The reach cast is of most importance. Every float fisher should master this simple technique, because one can achieve up to three times the length of a dead-drifted fly by using it. Whether you are fishing dry flies, nymphs, or even streamers, this technique should improve your catch rate.

THE REACH CAST

The way to get the longest drag-free drift of your fly while floating is to cast at a downstream angle using the reach cast. It's a very simple ploy but indispensable in many fishing situations. (See the illustration on page 118.)

Begin by making a straight overhead cast (not a sidearmed one) at about a 45-degree downstream angle. Make your cast a little higher than usual, with a bit of extra power. As your line begins to turn over above its intended landing site, slowly and smoothly reach your rod upstream as far as you comfortably can. This takes place before your line or fly

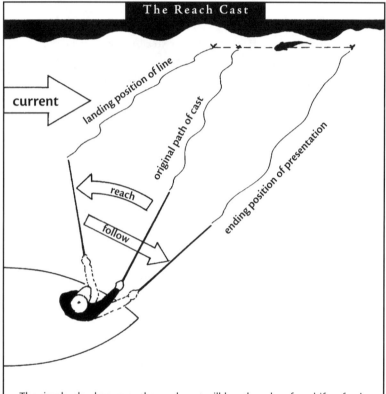

The Reach Cast

current

landing position of line

original path of cast

ending position of presentation

reach

follow

The simple ploy known as the reach cast will lengthen drag-free drifts of a dry fly or nymph severalfold. It allows streamers to sink deeper, as well. It should become float-fishing habit and used on almost every cast.

hits the water. After reaching your arm and rod upstream, and when the fly line and leader fully extend, drop your rod tip, line, and fly gently to the water. The fly should now go over fish before the leader does. (When a fish takes, you have to pause half a second before setting the hook, allowing the trout to head back under, otherwise you might pull the fly right out of the mouth of larger slow-rising trout.) As your line and fly float downstream, follow their progress with your rod tip. The cast lands with you reaching upstream, and you follow the fly until you're reaching downstream. This 15-plus feet of rod tip and arm movement allows very long drag-free drifts of a fly.

To add more slack, which is always a good idea at the beginning of a dry fly or nymph drift, a slightly more powerful forward cast can be made. Upon completely unfurling, the line will spring back a bit, creating some slack. This happens while you are reaching upstream. In some cases you'll want to cast beyond your targeted feed lane, for the reach and bounce-back effect will draw your fly back toward you somewhat.

For even more slack, your rod tip can be wiggled up and down while you make the reach. At the same time, release some extra line through your rod's guides. Now you should have plenty of slack built into the drift of line and fly for extralong drag-free drifts. These can be necessary for some rising-fish situations as well as when covering the water. They help immensely in thwarting drag when casting into bank eddies and across swirling eddy lines. When deep nymphing, long drifts allow the fly to sink to the proper level, for only then is it beginning to do its job. It's often advantageous to cast streamers on a slack line, too, letting them sink a while along a bank before retrieving. This helps get them deep. When trout are slow to move to a fly, dead-drifted deep streamers can work better than stripped ones.

Even good slack-line reach casts may need to be mended in the traditional fashion. The swifter water near the boat will want to belly your line downstream. Throwing a little upstream mend just after your fly lands is a good habit to develop. Roll line both upstream and toward the bank you're fishing while releasing more line through your rod's guides. This keeps from putting tension on the line and leader that's already on the water, which would pull out the slack you created and drag your fly. Mends should always be done as anticipatory maneuvers, not as last-ditch efforts.

STACK MENDS

The ultimate long drift combines an extreme reach cast with stack mends. These are coils of slack that are flipped out as soon as your fly line lands, in anticipation of achieving that very long drift.

Stack mends are made by flipping several loose lengths of fly line toward the fly and its intended path. Drop your rod tip low and use quick little up-and-out flicks of the tip to propel extra line in the direction of your fly. I believe up-and-down wiggles are better than side-to-side ones. They aren't usually rolled upstream, as most mends are. The end result is a lot of slack line on the water that slowly straightens out as boat and fly line float downstream. I use this method most when indicator nymphing, and when fishing two-fly rigs, hoppers, and attractor drys. Superlong drifts can allow a better overall coverage of the water when one is fishing blind. Sometimes stack mends are needed to sneak a fly over a rising fish, too, especially from extreme upstream angles.

Should a trout take your fly just after you stack mend a lot of slack on the water, a comic scene can follow. Anglers are seen stripping line in like mad while leaning backward until they almost fall over. It can be difficult to tighten up and set the hook. The rower can help tighten your line a little by quickly rowing away from the fish. I'll also set the hook by mending line in such a situation. A big power mend or two that throws your line toward midriver can get rid of all the slack and set the hook at the same time. If you mend quickly and vigorously enough, the trout will be hooked with the midriver currents dragging your line and keeping tension on the fish while you reel up on him until you make direct line contact. It's not foolproof, but it often works for me.

TUCK CASTS

The aim of the tuck cast is to make the fly land before the line and leader. This allows longer drifts of a dry fly, especially in swirling bank eddies. It's achieved by overpowering the forward cast while keeping it a little higher over the water than usual (just like the bounce-back reach cast—the two can be combined). The line rapidly turns over, straightens, then is carried by momentum to turn the fly under the main length of fly line. A fly can hit the water a second or two before the fly line falls, which can be just long enough to get an eddy fish to slurp it in. Big wind-resistant dry flies won't tuck as easily but can be jammed into a tuck with an enthusiastic power cast. A little tug or haul on the fly line applied just as the forward cast begins to turn over and straighten will accelerate line speed, enhancing the tuck effect.

Any time the fly lands before the line, or at least at the same time, longer drag-free drifts can be achieved. When a fly line slowly unfurls across the water with the fly landing last, the line will already be bellying downstream before the fly even hits the water. This effect is particularly noticeable in float-fishing due to the swift currents nearest angler and boat.

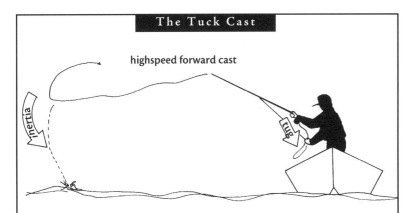

The Tuck Cast

highspeed forward cast

inertia

tug

An overpowered forward cast shot out at about shoulder level will turn line and fly over, then under, the main length of your fly line. A tug or haul made with your line hand just as your fly is about to turn over will increase line speed and enhance the effect. (Adding this third haul to a double-haul cast makes it a great wind-fighting tool. The triple haul both punches line out *and* helps force the fly down to the spot you were aiming for before the wind blows it away!) Wind-resistant dry flies are hard to tuck, but any time you can get the fly to land before the leader and line do from a boat, it will improve your chances of fooling a trout.

Another benefit of the tuck cast is that one is able to force a fly down with greater impact. This is useful when nymph-fishing. The added impetus helps sink a nymph all the quicker. Same goes for streamers. Some particularly ferocious trout will pounce on a streamer that's slapped down several feet from them (but not if it lands on their heads). That same forceful impact helps imitate hoppers, too. The splashdown can bring fish racing over to ingest. Real hoppers often land hard and from a high altitude; they can land anywhere across a big river. Others just tumble in from bankside grasses.

One can combine a tuck cast with a reach cast, too, although the act of reaching can pull the tuck right out of it. If you release slack through your rod's guides while reaching, some tuck can be maintained. This is an excellent way to fish bank eddies from the boat when casting at a downstream angle. The tuck cast will help presentations from all angles, though, and is worth practicing.

There are of course other casts and manipulations that can be used when float-fishing, just as when wading. Sidearm casts might skip and sneak a fly under overhanging willows. Double- and triple-haul casts help shoot line farther faster, and help keep it from getting blown away in a big wind. Hauling also takes a lot of work off your rod arm while also helping to project flies high and safely above your boatmates.

On the whole, though, it's the slack-line reach cast that's the floating angler's most-used tool. Some regular mends will still be necessary to keep line from bellying and flies from dragging. One habitual good mend just after the line is laid out on a reach cast helps insure a longer float.

A simple trick beginners can use if their control is less than perfect is to skid a fly into the correct feed lane. They can cast down and across and try to get their fly beyond a rising trout's feed lane. The rod tip is then lifted high and swung back upstream (similar to reaching) until the fly skids into the trout's lane. When it gets to the lane, the rod tip is lowered near the water and pointed toward the fly. This gives a novice a long-enough drag-free float to fool many trout. The skid should take place just before the fly is in the trout's view, say 4–6 feet upstream of it. This should produce a dead drift of 10 feet or so, enough to do the job and do it well. Naturally, a fly that floats well aids the process, one that doesn't routinely sink when skidded.

The skid to create slack ploy can be used in other situations, too, and also merely to lengthen the drag-free drift of a hopper or attractor dry. When a fly starts swinging and dragging at the end of your initial presentation, and if it's still going over a premium zone, a lift, reach, and skid will rejuvenate the dead drift for a little while longer. You can do it repeatedly, too, if your fly keeps floating.

You might have a fly drifting out near the bank and then see a trout rise to your side of it. A quick skid can line up your fly with the feed lane without a recast. Such little manipulations of rod, line, and fly come in handy for many things.

UNSNAGGING A FLY FROM THE BOAT

One of those little things the line can be made to do is unsnag a fly that's caught on a stream edge or shallow rock. It must be done as soon as the fly is snagged, before the boat floats any farther downstream. I call this maneuver the unsnagging roll cast.

First, rip a little extra line off your reel. Now make an extra powerful and high roll cast. The object is to propel your fly line and leader beyond your fly's position. It may take a couple of attempts to get your line up and far enough over the snag to do the trick. Ultimately, the roll cast that goes beyond your fly pulls it from behind and usually unsnags it.

This technique doesn't work for flies tangled in bushes, however. The thing to do here is just to pull slowly and steadily on the line. The fly may creep its way out of the limbs. Any rash jerking of the line tends to worsen the situation or break off the fly. Always check your leader for frays after encounters with foliage, rocks, or other snags.

You may have to row over to undo some snags, or perhaps just break off your fly. When rowing over to a snag, you may come to a point where it's difficult to continue to row because the bankside oar will have become incapacitated by the shore. The crawl stroke can be used to get closer than conventional rowing allows. If there are protruding bushes, these tend to get caught up in the bank oar, too. In areas of swift water, the angler may have just a second to unsnag the fly. The best procedure is to break off the limb that the fly's tangled on and extricate it at leisure in the boat. Watch your rod and line during this quick-grab operation. It's quite common for people to actually worsen the situation by concentrating on their fly while forgetting which way their rod is pointing. Their rod and fly line end up getting more tangled than the fly originally was. I see this all the time. Rods are occasionally broken, too. Put your rod down and point it the other way before going in to rescue your fly along a swift-water bank. Be careful not to snag the fly in your hand if the boat drifts off. One can also anchor near the snag and sometimes be able to reach it from the boat, at other times the angler must get out and walk. Make sure the location in which you stop is suitable both for anchoring and wading. I prefer to break my fly off rather than interrupt other anglers' fishing and make more work for the rower. Always bring a good supply of flies, and expect to lose some along the way.

Float-Fishing Tackle

Most anglers prefer 8½–9-foot, 4–6-weight rods constructed of relatively high-modulus graphite. These have the length and power to pick your fly line crisply off the water and propel it high and safely over the heads of your boatmates. These tools can also punch line out into the wind and throw big heavy flies, yet also drop #20 drys with finesse. Today's 9-foot 5-weight high-modulus rod can do almost anything. You can bring a heavier 7–8-weight for serious big-fly work, and a lighter 3–4-weight for those perfect calmish days when trout rise well.

Most anglers like weight-forward lines. They cast farther faster and can punch into breezes. When floating by hot spots, the ability to get casts out quickly counts. A sinking-tip line is handy for streamer fishing and also punches out into a wind well. Many anglers bring two rods on a float trip, one for dry flies and another for heavier wets. It's quicker to change rods than to rerig one. Fishing situations can change often as you float a river: a rising fish here, a good-looking nymph drop-off there. Keep the extra rod protected when it's not in use. Many are broken every year and in every conceivable way!

Have leader and tippet materials down to 6X on hand. Leader length and strength demands vary from river to river. Picky tailwater trout might require 12-foot and longer leaders tapering to 6X. Swift-water backcountry trout might be easily caught on 7–9-foot leaders tapering to 4X.

Weights that can be attached to leaders, strike indicators, floatant, and fly-drying crystals should all be aboard, too. The latter are very handy, especially if one catches fish with regularity. Dry-fly crystals suck all the moisture from bedraggled flies, coat them with a layer of powdered floatant, and make them float like new.

A smooth-feeding reel is a good asset for hot running fish, though it's often more important when wading than when fishing from a boat, for following the fish with the boat tends to reduce any egregious ground-covering.

OTHER GEAR

A large boat net should be on board. Hemostats or needlenose pliers are handy for removing flies from fish, anchor ropes, and certain parts of the human anatomy. Don't forget raingear, hot- and cold-weather clothing, hat, sunglasses, sunscreen, lip balm, skin cream (days on arid and windy western rivers can really take it out of your skin), plus adequate nourishment and liquid refreshment. Have plenty of drinking water on hand for very hot days.

A good waterproof duffel bag is best for storing gear. Those with lengthwise openings are much easier to get in and out of, as compared to the old narrow-end-sealing white-water bags. Bring rod cases that also house reels to protect rods that aren't in use. Neoprene waders are good not only for insulated wading but also as raingear during cold thunderstorms (or summer snowstorms). I usually wear shorts and sandals in the boat and carry bootfoot neoprene waders for deep wading or rain. These are easy to get into and out of.

Life jackets, a first-aid kit and book, an extra oar, and throw rope should be on hand when floating, plus a patch kit and pump for rafts. A detailed river map is helpful if the rower is unfamiliar with the water: These are available for most rivers these days. Flashlights come in handy for late take-outs. Do have a spare set of keys for your shuttle vehicles! Don't forget to make your shuttle arrangements at the beginning of your trip.

In cold weather a thermos or two of hot soup or drink helps take the chill off. A small stove and hot lunch is a good idea, too. Prepared meals can be brought along. Have some fire starter and matches or lighter in case of hypothermia.

High-quality waterproof containers are widely available for cameras, first-aid kits, fire-starting gear, glasses, wallets, books, and what have you. You might want to bring an extra roll of film along, too—it might be a big-fish day!

Being prepared for any contingency is a little more work but a lot more satisfying than having your day ruined by inattention to detail. Forgetting raingear on a long day of cold rain, or neglecting to bring sunscreen on sunny days can create negative memories of float trips for novice floaters.

6

CHOOSING AND OUTFITTING
THE RIGHT BOAT

*S*electing a river drift boat is no simple matter these days. A growing industry is supplying recreational craft in more designs, sizes, materials, and prices than ever before. It seems like good drift boats have doubled in price in the last ten years. They've become a substantial investment for many, but one gladly made.

A prospective buyer has much to consider based on the water and wind conditions where he lives and plans to fish. White-water maneuvering demands, wind frequency and ferocity, the number of people one plans to fish with, storage capabilities, fishing comfort and stability, and price range are among the major considerations. Storage, transport options, and the quality or even presence of boat ramps on local waters bear some thought, too. An occasional floater might prefer the trunk-loading and easier storage option of a thousand-dollar raft. The hard-core frequent-floating addict tends to like the trailered readiness of a slick rigged drift boat (which can cost upwards of six thousand dollars these days). Let's consider some of the options.

Raft, Pram, or Drift Boat?

RAFTS

There are many makes and models of inflatables, or rafts, to choose from, most from 8–18 feet in length. Prices currently range from about six hundred to six thousand dollars. You get what you pay for where rafts are concerned. Most fishermen prefer 12–14-foot

Twelve-to-14-foot rafts are excellent choices for all-around river fishing due to their stability, shallow draft, and capacity for extra camping gear.

boats. Experienced boaters and quality-boat manufacturers speak of rafts in terms of feet in length and width and tube diameter, not as six- or eight-person rafts or what have you. Midsized rafts are easy to row, have acceptable room and storage capabilities, and will handle most any river situation short of monster holes and class V white water. Most midsize rafts cost between eight hundred and thirty-six hundred dollars for the bare boat. New rafts that cost less than this will be of pretty marginal quality over the long term. Hunting down a good used one is always a sensible option, especially if you're not in a hurry, for the availability of good used rafts is seldom very high.

In addition to the bare raft you'll need a rowing frame (at three to five hundred dollars), oars (around one hundred dollars each), plus seats, a pump, patch kit, a strong frame-fitting cooler (another sixty or more dollars), and ropes. An anchor system is a good idea, too. Few if any anchor systems are commercially available for rafts (manufacturers, please take the hint!). Custom-made front and rear knee braces and an anchor system for the ultimate fly-fishing raft cost two hundred or more dollars. Anchors go for around forty to fifty dollars.

On the plus side for rafts is their ability to be rolled up and transported in a vehicle without the added cost of a trailer, as well as the fact that they take up less storage space. Some frequent river runners do keep and transport rafts on trailers because it eliminates set-up and take-down time on stream.

Rafts have that built-in buoyancy that makes them a safer, more forgiving craft in demanding water situations. They also draw less water when floating and are the choice for some smaller shallow rivers, especially during late summer's low flows. I use rafts on some shallow rivers and drift boats on others, depending on water depth and launch-site quality or availability.

Rafts don't row quite as well as hard-hull boats. Nor are they as comfortable to stand up in and cast from. There are, however, modifications that can improve these deficits to some degree. Self-bailing rafts, which have inflated floors, row better than traditional models while allowing any water shipped from waves, rain, or dripping waders to drain. Knee braces can be custom-built to make standing to fish easier in rafts. Wooden floors can also be added to firm up the footing.

Raft design and materials bear consideration, too. White-water rafts tend to have larger-diameter tubes to increase buoyancy and fend off big waves. Upturning of the front and back ends is more pronounced for the same reason. These qualities don't hurt in a fishing boat except under one condition—wind. If you plan to fish where waters are mellow and wind can be high (much of Montana, for instance), a lower-profile raft might be a better choice.

The high bow upturn on some rafts makes them more comfortable to stand up in and lean against at the front of the boat, and it works to some degree as a knee brace. Lower-profile rafts don't have the same built-in knee-brace qualities, but they don't catch as much wind, either. It is these that benefit most from the addition of fabricated knee braces, which can be built on an extended rowing frame. Most design features carry performance trade-offs to some degree.

Catamaran rafts are another option, though anglers seem to show less interest in them than do white-water enthusiasts. In the smallest sizes they have come to replace float tubes as high-performance one-person fishing craft. Most use oars and swim fins for a dual-option maneuvering: oars for major ferries, fins for slowing and minor positioning while fishing.

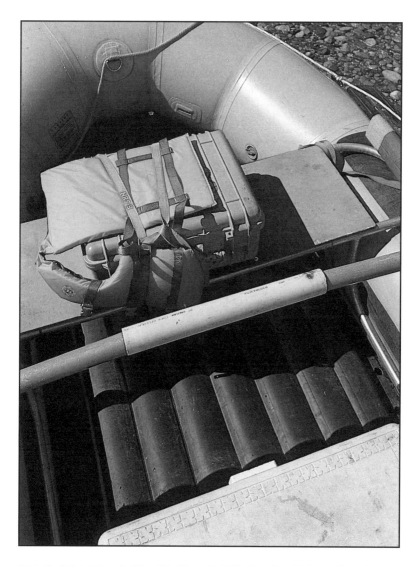

Note the inflated floor in this self-bailing raft. Self-bailers float higher and row better than conventional rafts, but they weigh and cost more.

Comparing Fishing Craft Designs

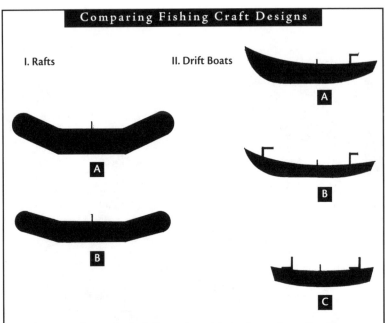

I. Rafts

II. Drift Boats

I. There are plenty of raft makes and models to choose from. Consider your local water, wind, and fishing conditions before choosing.

A. Rafts built for serious white water have larger-diameter tubes and greater upturn (rocker) fore and aft to better handle big water. They also catch more wind.

B. If mellower rivers twisting through breeze-frequented terrain are in your forecast, consider rafts with smaller tube diameters and less upturn. Self-bailing rafts will skim over shallower riffles more easily than conventional rafts.

II. Drift boats now come in a variety of designs, too. Smaller rowing prams add to your hard hull choices.

A. Traditional drift boats were built with serious white water in mind on the rough and tumble steelhead rivers of the West Coast. They're stable and comfortable to fish from but catch a lot of wind and are easier for trout to see on flat water.

B. Lower-profile drift boats can be better choices for many of the easy flowing trout rivers of the Rocky Mountain West, where the wind has been known to blow.

C. A variety of rowing prams make excellent choices, as well. They handle moderate water, weigh less, and have a low wind profile. Many lack knee braces though, and are not as easy or comfortable to stand up in and cast from.

Larger catamaran rafts of 12–18 feet (and on up to 35-foot monsters used to run the Grand Canyon) are available and somewhat popular in white-water circles. These weigh less, row well, obviously don't ship water, and fold up into relatively small packages. The rowing frame is by nature rather complex and thus pricey. It can have desired features built into it, including full-length floor, bow knee braces, and an anchor system. There are many builders of rowing frames who do custom jobs. The end product costs about 25 percent less than a fully rigged regular-quality raft and can be a viable option.

High-quality rafts are made from two basic material families: hypalon/neoprene and PVC, an advanced reinforced vinyl. The former was common in rafts for years. The higher the percentage of hypalon in the laminate, the longer-lived and better-made the raft tends to be. Avon rafts have always been leaders in the material quality and river boat fields, though many other manufacturers build high-quality products, some of which are better designed for certain uses and cost less than Avons.

The other material that's come into prominence in the last decade is reinforced PVC laminate. Improvements in materials, bonding, and design have helped boats made of this material get a big market share of late. These aren't the flimsy vinyl boats you may be thinking of; they're priced right up there with hypalon rafts, though some are significantly cheaper. One feature of PVC boats is their greater rigidity when inflated. This translates into a raft that rows more like a hard-hull boat while keeping its shape in severe turbulence. PVC boats don't buckle as much as hypalon boats do in big holes. White-water floaters like the improved handling characteristics of a stiff PVC boat. Anglers can take advantage of that rowing benefit, too. The self-bailing models row particularly well.

All in all, rafts are the best choice for many float fishers, depending on frequency and location of use, stream depth, potential white-water use, ramp availability, and camp-cargo hauling capabilities. They save the cost of a trailer and can be stored in a small area (out of the sun's harmful rays). They're forgiving in demanding water, can bounce off obstacles, and are more likely to make it through misguided rowing adventures than other craft are. A raft package can be

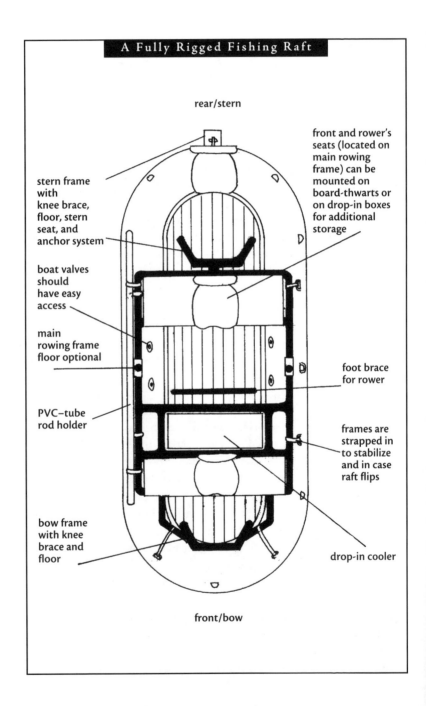

A Fully Rigged Fishing Raft

rear/stern

front and rower's seats (located on main rowing frame) can be mounted on board-thwarts or on drop-in boxes for additional storage

stern frame with knee brace, floor, stern seat, and anchor system

boat valves should have easy access

main rowing frame floor optional

foot brace for rower

PVC–tube rod holder

frames are strapped in to stabilize and in case raft flips

bow frame with knee brace and floor

drop-in cooler

front/bow

Fishing boats can be built on inflatable catamaran tubes. These craft cost less but can carry less overall cargo than conventional rafts. They maneuver well, though, are lightweight, and would make good one- or two-person fishing craft.

bought for less than a pram or drift boat; consequently, rafts remain the most popular floating choice in the West.

PRAMS

Modern rowing prams are something of a cross between full-sized drift boats (with their pronounced rocker, or bottom curvature) and flat-bottomed johnboats. Most are a little shorter than drift boats, with somewhat lower sides, especially in the front end. Some are a lot like a drift boat, with 2 feet cut off the nose. Their square-ended look is perhaps less aesthetically pleasing than that of a drift boat but better fits the rowing requirements of many waters. Most have modified rocker and maneuver very well because of a lowered wind profile. This alone can be important. The lighter weight, efficient use of space, slightly smaller size, low wind profile, and excellent handling properties have made prams a popular choice among today's recreational anglers and guides. Although they are not cheap by any means, they are less expensive than full-sized 16–17-foot drift boats. Some one- to two-person prams have even been designed to fit

Rafts of 14–16 feet are the best choices for those planning many overnight expeditions and white-water trips. They can carry much more gear, will draw less water when loaded compared to a smaller raft, and handle big water well.

in the bed of a standard pickup truck and are just lightweight enough to lift onto one. Prams range in size from these smaller, 8–10-foot craft on up to 16 feet. The smallest ones seem most popular on mellower stretches of West Coast salmon rivers, where "big-fish fever" makes river addicts out of many. Fourteen-foot models are quite popular on Rocky Mountain trout rivers, and the larger models add more storage capacity and overnighting potential. Though some small to midsized prams could be "car topped," most are trailered for ease of use.

Float fishers who ply rivers with little or no real white water could find rowing prams to be an ideal choice. The only down side to some of them is that they lack the knee braces found in most drift boats, which make standing to cast a pleasure. It is easy to fall out of a pram if one is standing unsupported. However, braces can be added by inventive owners in both bow and stern. Many homemade stern knee braces also incorporate a backrest for the rower's seat, which otherwise is not usually found. This adds some back comfort for boatmen spending long days on the river.

Rowing prams have squared-off ends, like johnboats, but they also have the rocker, or end-to-end curvature, of a drift boat. This allows them to maneuver well in moving water. They catch less wind, too. Most are 12–14 feet in length and have become top choices as western fishing craft.

Because most prams are a little smaller than full-sized drift boats, they have a little less storage space. Most are well designed, though, and adequate for day use. Anchor systems are generally included in the purchase package.

In big water or heavy rapids a raft or drift boat would be a safer choice, but a rowing pram's handling characteristics allow it to be navigated through challenging stretches quite well. Ultimately, a pram would be a little easier to capsize, especially in the hands of a novice rower. On the mellower trout rivers in many western states, though, today's prams command a large share of the float-fishing market.

One other benefit of lower-sided prams is their reduced visibility to fish. They're also easy to get in and out of when wade-fishing in waders. High-sided drift boats with standing anglers spook fish sooner where waters are flat and fishing pressure is high. Trout can see them from farther away, so drift-boat anglers sometimes have to cast farther to overcome this handicap. Prams with seated anglers allow a closer approach to fish. Dull earth-tone hull colors are better choices than bright white or brilliant colors. With the growing fishing pressure on most rivers these days, every advantage helps. Staying low and out of sight isn't a bad place to start.

DRIFT BOATS

The generic name "drift boat," apparently adopted for lack of a better term, usually designates river dories of various designs. Some people call any river dory a McKenzie boat. This, too, is imprecise, because the McKenzie boat is just a localized design common to the Oregon river of the same name and as a craft is quite different in form from most other dories.

The dory is an ancient design that is widely used in seas and oceans around the world. Its adaptation to river use (with an increased rocker for maneuvering) came in the late 1800s on coastal Oregon rivers, where white water and big fish coincide. Over the course of the century they became an accepted craft on swift trout, salmon, and steelhead rivers across the West. They're now even seen Back East, in New Zealand, and on other rivers worldwide.

Several manufacturers build dories of fiberglass, aluminum, and wood. Each material offers some advantage. Drift boats of 13–17 feet are most commonly constructed, with 14–16-foot models being most popular. (Dories are traditionally measured along the gunwales and not down the center. A 16-foot board, for instance, was bent to shape the sides of a boat, thus the boat was a 16-footer. The center line itself would be closer to 15 feet.) Its stability, maneuverability, fishing comfort, and style make the drift boat a welcome addition to many a river angler's arsenal, and next to his Suburban, pickup truck, or Explorer, perhaps the most expensive.

On the plus side for drift boats are their ability to handle rough water, the stand-up fishing comfort of their knee braces, ample storage space, and excellent rowing qualities. They have rocker for maneuvering in fast water, respond well to the crawl stroke, and can be rowed to a standstill in a good current. Most come with anchor systems, seats with backrests, and other options with anglers in mind. Rear knee braces are becoming more common options, too, which is good, because it's the stern angler who sometimes falls out of the boat! Winter steelheaders even put propane heaters in drift boats. The best ones have graceful lines and a stylish look. Prices now range

River dories, or drift boats, have become the standard craft on many western rivers, and especially where swift water and waves come into play. They're comfortable to fish from, but they do catch wind.

from thirty-five hundred to sixty-five hundred dollars, including trailer. Build-it-yourself wood-boat kits with precut parts can be bought for just under one thousand dollars.

On the negative side, drift boats generally require a reasonable ramp from which to launch and take out (though it's easier to slide one down a bank than it is to pull it back up). Most weigh close to 300 pounds, a little much to bust brush with. Many rivers have adequate ramps, so this won't be a problem in most locales. Exploratory types who shun crowds might want to stick with rafts or other light craft that make nonramp put-ins much easier.

Drift boats are a little hard to get in and out of, especially for the less agile. If a party stops often to get out and wade-fish, this could present a problem for some anglers wearing waders. In this situation a raft would probably be easiest to get in and out of and a pram would be easier, too. I've often wondered why manufacturers don't build a watertight door in the front end of drift boats because this area is above the waterline. This would be easy to do and would certainly make getting in and out of the boat easier, especially in midstream at wadable gravel bars. I think it's just one of those simple ideas that seem to take humans forever to figure out!

On small shallow rivers drift boats can draw too much water for easy navigation. A drift boat with three people and gear draws 10–12 inches of water. A raft or johnboat with a similar load draws only half that. You can beat, dent, and chip the heck out of a drift boat's hull during a day's drift on a too-shallow river. A pram is better in shallow water, and a raft is better yet.

Although drift boats are usually the most expensive river rowing craft (some rafts and prams are right up there in price, too), they usually last a long time and have good resale value if maintained. Used drift boats in my area are snapped up quickly because so few seem to be available at any one time.

Last but certainly not least on the negative side is the drift boat's great ability to catch wind. It will sail like a leaf in middling blows and become difficult to control in your every-third-day, east-slope-of-the-Rockies chinook gale. Forty to 60 mph gusts keep experienced boatmen on their toes and get novices into blister- and callus-building high gear! Getting blown into banks or navigational hazards is a distinct possibility for beginners in drift boats. Some manufactures and designs are better or worse than others. There are extrahigh-sided ones built with white water in mind (which are not so good in the wind), and low-sided ones now being targeted at mellower but windy trout rivers. Those fishing more sheltered river valleys with some white water prefer the high-sided models. Here in Montana's big wind country ("big sky" is just a cover up), low-sided models are often preferred. High-sided drift boats with rolled gunwales are the worst for wind in my experience. This is a construction feature of some fiberglass boats that eases the task of manufacture but catches additional wind. Bear these factors in mind when it's time to choose a boat.

Aluminum, Fiberglass, or Wood?: Drift Boat and Pram Construction Options

Three basic materials are used to build river rowing craft: aluminum, fiberglass laminates, and wood. Each material has its devotees

Lower-sided drift boats with front and rear knee braces are finally becoming readily available. These well-equipped craft are better suited to many windy western rivers than their traditional brethren.

and detractors. Aluminum and fiberglass are chosen most perhaps for their low maintenance requirements, but there are some other reasons.

ALUMINUM

Aluminum drift boats are favored by many, and especially by steelhead and salmon fishermen of the Northwest, for their durability. Where rock-slamming white water and big waves are daily occurrences, aluminum seems to be the material of choice. Good aluminum drift boats aren't cheap but should give a lifetime of service, disasters aside. Wrapped drift boats can even be straightened and welded back into serviceable condition, something that's not as likely to happen with glass and wood boats.

Negative qualities of aluminum boats include noise. Water lapping against the hull makes a faint ringing sound, and anything dropped in the boat can alarm fish by the transmitted sound. This minor irritant can be overcome with the installation of some outdoor carpet on the floor and a little way up the insides.

Aluminum sticks to rocks more than glass or wood, should the boat be high-centered. The rock will bite into the aluminum a bit, especially coarse or jagged rocks, bringing the boat to a halt on top of barely submerged midstream rock. In some cases the water around such a rock will be so deep that you can't get out of the boat to push it off. A combination of rocking, oar levering, spinning, and hard rowing is then needed to break free. There are paint-on hull treatments such as Gluv-it to help alleviate this problem. Though they are quite pricey per gallon, many aluminum-boat owners use these treatments to coat their hulls.

Another complaint one hears about aluminum is its easy transmission of temperature. Cold water can make cold the aluminum in which you're spending your day. Modern insulated clothing minimizes this annoyance. Winter steelheaders carry small portable propane heaters for angling comfort.

Uncoated aluminum can leave a grayish residue on hands and clothes. This, too, is a small point, because the seats are usually made of a different material. Many aluminum boats come painted, or at least have coated gunwales and knee braces.

This West Coast steelhead drift boat is fitted with an awning to fend off those North-ern California rains, and no doubt a propane heater for winter use. Such an awning would probably capsize the craft on windy Rocky Mountain rivers!

Most problems aside, aluminum remains a top choice for prams and drift boats, especially where hull abuse can be expected.

FIBERGLASS

This maintenance-free material is popular due to its ease of manufacture, moldability, longevity, and moderate price. Although there are expensive "tricked-out" fiberglass drift boats on the market, other basic models are the lowest-priced new drift boats to be found.

Even though fiberglass is maintenance-free, it will ultimately last longer and look better if it is kept out of the sun when not in use. Sunshine is the enemy of synthetics and most exterior finishes. A boat cover is desirable, a garage better yet. Although sun damage to the actual laminate would take decades to appear, color fading of the exterior gel coat and interior paint will be noticeable much sooner.

Fiberglass has one advantage over other materials, that of slid-ing over rocks with greater ease. Some models are designed to allow the floor to flex, further facilitating this sliding, nontipping benefit. Too much rock hopping and floor flexing will begin to deteriorate the laminate's rigidity, though. It's not something you want to take to extremes.

Although fiberglass can puncture and chip and is more likely to break up in serious collisions and wraps, most glass boats are built so heavily in the hull as to make daily wear and tear inappreciable, even over a long period of time. Fiberglass is also the easiest boat material to repair. A boat can even be quickly patched riverside, should the owner have the foresight to carry a fiberglass patch kit. (The same patch kit can repair a wood boat, too. Duct tape even works for small jobs as a quick fix.)

Some fiberglass drift boats are the ugly ducklings of the riverboat world. Although they are utilitarian enough, it's hard to ignore their tubby, homely look. Others are more graceful and pleasing to the eye, though the splatter paint used on the interior of most fiberglass boats never has turned me on. Its purpose of hiding both dirt and manufacturer's flaws and rough edges just gives a cheap look to the finished product, to my mind. This is especially true of boats that are 100 percent fiberglass. Some models feature wood gunwales and trim, which adds a more sophisticated look. A person who can't find the time to rub oil or to paint on one coat of finish a year to a gunwale is probably too busy to fish anyway!

Some high-sided, rolled-gunwale fiberglass boats seem to be worst of all in wind. The rolled gunwale catches a little more wind than a straight one does, making a boat lurch over in strong side winds. A leaning boat is hard to row because the oar tends to hit the low-side knee. Whether made so by wind or leaning humans, a heeled-over drift boat is difficult or impossible to row. And although no river boat is much fun in the wind, some are certainly worse than others. Rolled gunwales could be cut off some models by the industrious and replaced with wood (ash is best). This should improve wind resistance a little and looks a lot.

Although not ultimately as repairable as aluminum after a major wrap, fiberglass boats have few other downsides. What remain are usually design weaknesses rather than material flaws. Check the market for hull designs, seat and storage options, front and rear knee braces, anchor systems, color options, and the like.

Good boats have adjustable seat positions so that the boat will trim out properly, whether two or three people are in the craft. A drift boat that plows water with the stern when someone's sitting aft is

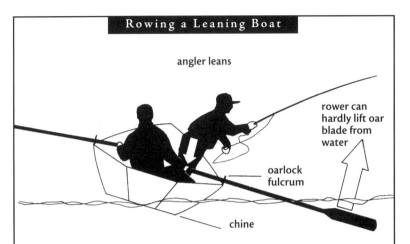

Rowing a Leaning Boat

angler leans

rower can hardly lift oar blade from water

oarlock fulcrum

chine

When a drift boat is leaning too far to one side (usually because the bow angler is leaning too far to one side and not keeping centered!), the rower can hardly pick the oar blade up out of the water, for the oar handle now hits his knee. And because the hull is no longer flat on the water, the chine now acts as a curved centerboard, disrupting the boat's forward drift. These two elements combined make a leaning drift boat or pram *very* difficult to row. Wind and white water sometimes produce the same oar handle and knee conflict. In some boats this situation can be improved if the oarlock position is slightly raised.

harder to row. This is a design flaw that many manufacturers seem to have no interest in correcting, and a very stupid one. Water should not hit the stern, it should slide under it and hit only the bottom, even with an angler seated in the back. Many boats have their sterns lifted free of the water when an angler in the back of the boat stands up to fish and leans into a rear knee brace. This is how most boats with two casters and a boatman row best, *if* the anglers are secure in knee braces and not falling around the boat!

WOOD

There are certainly many devotees of good wooden river boats. "Hey, nice-looking boat" is something you don't hear much when rowing fiberglass or aluminum. The beauty of clear finished wood on water is undeniable. And it doesn't need as much maintenance as some people think if it's built right in the first place and kept out of the elements when not in use. The sun is the enemy of a wooden boat's finish!

What really makes wood a realistic option, even for low-maintenance devotees, is epoxy saturation. A boat that's well built from the right types of wood (those that water doesn't hurt, like ash, spruce, cedar, and quality marine ply) and that's coated, sealed, or fiberglassed with epoxy will last a long time without much refinishing. A recreational weekend floater who keeps his boat fully covered or garaged should be able to go several years between cosmetic varathane applications over the epoxy base. Heavily used parts like gunwales, knee braces, and seats might need a coat of varathane or other hard exterior sun-resistant finish once a season. Any punctures or serious abrasions should be treated immediately, of course, to preserve the wood. Nylon skid plates are a worthwhile option for the bottom of wooden boats plied on more abrasive rivers.

Most of the minor damage to my eighteen-year-old cedar drift boat came from the few times I loaned it out. If someone asks to borrow it now I just walk away laughing! Rowers of good wooden boats are more likely to avoid rocks than other floaters are, which only goes toward truly mastering rowing skills.

Wooden boats are less-likely candidates for serious rock-slamming rivers, for obvious reasons. Although a wooden boat can be built structurally to take it, one should expect more frequent refinishing and repair jobs. Many of Montana's trout rivers are gravel- and cobble-bottomed. A skilled rower rarely has to hit anything; my boat is eighteen years old now and has almost no real bottom wear. The chines, where bottom and sides meet, take the most abuse. I've reinforced mine twice over the years with the simple addition of a layer of fiberglass tape and epoxy.

Some wooden one- to two-person prams fit in the beds of pickups and are light enough to lift. "Cedar strip" and cross-laminated cedar-veneer boats are particularly light and epoxy-sealed. They can weigh half as much as plywood, fiberglass, or aluminum boats. Using the latest wood-construction technology, one could even build a 16-foot drift boat that weighs in at just over 100 pounds! If your rivers are "user easy" on boats and ramps are scarce, a 60–200-pound pram

High-quality epoxy-built wooden boats take less upkeep than you might imagine if they are kept out of the elements when not in use.

or drift boat is much easier to muscle around than a 300-pound fiberglass one.

There is a latent pleasure in building and maintaining your own wooden craft. When you've sanded and finished every beautiful grain and seen it reflect across the water in every light, it deepens the river experience that much more. Just like tying your own flies, building your own boat takes you deeper into the river world.

Wooden boats are not for everybody, but the technology is there to allow you to buy or build low-maintenance and beautiful wooden craft. I for one hate to see the whole world go plastic, and I see boaters who refuse to do any maintenance even though it means a much more beautiful possession. Wood boats row well, have a great feel in the water, and can have extremely long lives when maintained. They are by nature expensive when new (and sometimes dirt cheap when old and neglected), but your hours on the water seem more pleasurable on wood. Wooden boat kits can be bought for around one thousand dollars.

Rigging the Craft

Properly outfitting a boat enhances its fishability and comfort. Neat arrangements that don't tangle fly lines and have plenty of storage for gear and food are desirable. Anchor systems are a great asset, along with comfortable seating and knee braces. A well-rigged craft makes for a pleasurable day astream.

RAFTS

Rafts are often sold with no accessories other than a pump and patch kit. Rowing frames, oars, oar locks, and seats are extra. Boat dealers often offer raft and frame packages. It's a good idea to look at a number of them and scan the catalogs to see what's available before buying. You'd hate to buy one rowing frame (at two hundred to five hundred dollars) and then see one you like much better!

Rowing frames are your biggest consideration and expense after the raft itself. They vary in size, weight, materials, and design. Some have floors, which are good for storing gear and protecting the floor of your raft, some don't. Floors add more weight, so if weight is a major consideration (as when flying, horsepacking, or carrying equipment into a wilderness or rampless river), aluminum floorless frames are a wise choice. I've seen relatively lightweight homemade frames made of PVC plumbing pipe. Frames may be made from bent and welded conduit. Heavy homemade wooden ones are old standbys but now waning in popularity as the prefab market becomes more diverse. Whether homemade, catalog-chosen, or custom-built, it pays to consider how a rowing frame can best serve your needs.

Rowing frames serve several purposes. First and foremost, they stiffen the raft and provide a solid base from which to row. Be aware that the little rubber oar locks that come glued to the tubes of some cheaper rafts aren't very good performers in demanding rowing situations. Frames provide seating structure for the rower and bow angler. Frames also hold coolers for food and drink. Some are designed to house drop-in storage boxes for gear. These may be included with a frame and, of course, add to its cost. One handy arrangement is to have drop-in boxes (which can be carried up to a camp or into your house for loading) with seats on top. Any time you have gear serving double duty you come out ahead. Frames provide storage decks for things that would otherwise fall off the raft's round tubes, ending up wet on the floor or in the river. Frames with built-in solid floors add storage capability and comfort for standing while protecting the raft floor from puncture and abrasion.

There should be no weight on the raft floor itself; it must be able to stretch up and over rocks. Any weight sitting on the raft floor acts like an anvil or cutting board: The raft floor is cut or punctured between the weight on top of it and the river rocks underneath. That is why rowing-frame floors are important. A full-length floor can be built, though it will become rather heavy. Weight might be less of a consideration for some than optimal storage capabilities. One could even sleep on a full-length floor and design a tent that sets up on the raft frame. This would eliminate the need to set camp for one- or two-person trips.

The ultimate raft set-up would include an anchor system and rear knee braces. These aren't readily available and might have to be custom-made. The whole raft and frame industry is historically more concerned with white water than with fishing.

Different types of seats can be attached to a raft frame. Folding, padded, sturdy models are best for use and transport. Some are built on pedestals to give casters a little extra height (which makes the rower feel safer!).

Traditionally, raft frames didn't have anchor systems or knee braces. Anglers added them themselves or had them custom-made. You may still have to do this today. Two- or even three-part frames are seen: the main center frame in its traditional form, a stern frame with seat and anchor system, and a front piece for a knee brace. A rear knee brace could be built on either the main or rear frame. A full-length frame incorporating all these features can be built if transport and storage aren't a problem. Break-down frames are made, too. They brake down into several pieces for transport but always seem a bit of a pain to put back together. Stern frames are made to house motors and gas tanks, but rafts need to be stiffened for motorization. Even then they can only handle smaller engines. Those specifically designed to use a motor have strong built-in transoms but aren't well designed for rowing rivers unless they are rowed backwards.

Other accessories for rafts can be used when no stern angler is present. Cargo decks made of webbing and nets to tie down gear are popular. A big folding table can be lashed to the back of the boat for camping, and gear can be piled on top of it. A cargo rain cover could be made, though most floaters use a folded camp tarp under the netting to do the job. These are tied down to D rings that come built into the raft and the rowing frame. Cargo decks are useful for camping trips and, on smaller rafts, for day trips if only one angler is present. I have a 10-foot raft I'll use for two-person trips that can be transported in a compact car. With the rising price of gas, this can become an issue for some. It's a lot cheaper to Honda the raft than to pull the drift boat with my pickup! Such boats are light enough for one person to carry.

One last desirable accessory is a rod holder. Many floaters tie in a 9-foot length of PVC pipe along the outsides of their rafts, using the D rings as tie downs. Extra rods can be safely stored this way. Be sure to add some securing device, because I have seen rods work their way out of such tubes over time and slide out into the river. It *is* handy to have a second rod rigged with an alternative fly, though. The less clutter around the boat (as, for instance, a bunch of rod cases) the fewer tangles you'll have to fool with throughout the day.

PRAMS

Most prams are smaller than full-sized drift boats and economize somewhat on storage and knee braces. Most have three seats and an anchor system. Smaller models may have only two seats. There are even one-person models around, popular on mellower West Coast salmon rivers.

The addition of homemade knee braces isn't too difficult for the do-it-yourselfer. Many prams don't come with them. Some type of sturdy wood set-up is easy enough to figure out and attach. Otherwise, hunt the market for models that do have them.

Additional storage can be added to some models by affixing removable waterproof boxes under the thwarts (seat supports), except where pedestal seat mounts are used. A rod holder of some sort is always a good idea.

Most prams and drift boats have anchor systems. These feed the rope up to the rower's position via pulleys or a floor-mounted tube. They have either a jam cleat or more sophisticated self-locking foot-release mechanism within easy reach so the rower can control everything. Some anchor systems feed the rope up the side, others up the floor at the centerline. Most boaters seem to prefer the floor-mounted, foot-release automatic rope-locking models these days. The anchor can be released while the craft is being rowed, allowing the boatman to perfectly position the boat for anchoring in range of rising fish. When the anchor is pulled in the rower just lets go of the rope as it automatically jams. He doesn't have to manually jam the rope in a cleat. The only negative aspects to this system are that the rope piled on the floor can tangle a bit on its way out. In freezing weather, ice may inhibit the rope from passing through the narrow tube that feeds it to the stern pulleys. I have the older-system side-led rope and jam cleat. It serves me well enough—rowers tend to adapt to the equipment at hand. By the way, the anchor is lowered, not dropped. It can splash a seated stern angler. Once it has entered the water it can then be fully released.

Anchors vary in weight and design to meet the demands of different bottom types. An average weight would be 30 pounds. The most common design is probably the inverted pyramid. It bites into bottom strata well enough and isn't too likely to get snagged. Sand and fine gravel bottoms allow digging-type designs, which can be lighter in weight. Some of these look like mini–ship anchors, others are thinner and more streamlined. Avoid the cheap plastic-coated ones to be found in many department stores. The plastic coating doesn't allow the anchor to pivot on its stem as it should, thus negating its bottom-digging abilities. On swift bouldery rivers like Montana's Madison, some heavier-duty anchors may be seen. One design features a heavy horizontal cylinder with big metal studs sticking out in all directions. It would make a London punk rocker feel right at home on the boat! This anchor grabs the rounded stones well without snagging. There are of course other designs around, including such homemade mainstays as sections of railroad track and large coffee cans filled with cement or lead with an eyebolt molded in. Any big hunk of scrap metal or chain can work wherever snagging isn't a problem.

The anchor rope should be of high quality, soft and thick enough to be comfortable on the hands and not tangle as it goes through the pulleys. Avoid harsh-textured rope, especially the cheap

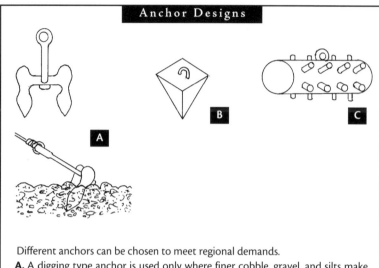

Different anchors can be chosen to meet regional demands.
A. A digging type anchor is used only where finer cobble, gravel, and silts make up the bottom structure. It will snag in rocks. One can use a lighter-weight anchor, though, because the digging "bite" enhances its hold.
B. The inverted pyramid is a common and good all-around anchor. Thirty pounds is a typical weight for a full-size drift boat.
C The studded cylinder is used on rounded-boulder rivers like Montana's Madison. It may even need to be overweighted, say 35–40 pounds.

yellow polypropylene stuff seen in most department stores. It stretches, has memory, and gets coils and kinks in it. It's rough on the hands, too. Tight, sophisticated weaves of polypropylene are best. They're memory-free, easy on the hands, and don't stretch. They cost a little more per foot but are well worth it, as you'll discover after lifting and dropping the anchor hundreds of times. About 30–35 feet of rope should do. Tie a knot in your end so it can't accidentally run out through the pulleys and be lost. It should be as thick as possible yet still glide freely through the pulleys and floor tube. The only minor downside to these tight-weave ropes is that it can be very difficult to unsnag a barbed fly from them. Believe me, a few *will* be left in place there!

Most boaters affix a quick-release attachment of some kind to the anchor end of the rope. Many prefer to remove the anchor for transport. Others just pull some rope out and lay the anchor in the boat. It can bounce around there just enough to do a little cosmetic damage, heavy though it is. Some boaters just let it dangle from the anchor system during transportation. It's not too unusual to see a rig take off down the road dragging the anchor on a length of rope behind the trailer. The boater is last seen heading into the sunset with the anchor swinging wildly from side to side.

Boaters sometimes forget to rope in the anchor after landing and trailering their craft. This is a more common scenario than you might imagine, so be sure to stow your anchor before loading. I had a bad habit of losing an anchor every year or so by leaving it at the take-out. I'd unhook it from the rope, lay it on the ground while packing up, and forget to pick it up, because the dull gray color can be difficult to spot at a twilight ramp. Always double check the ground around the ramp area, plus the top of your vehicle (where anglers sometimes put rods), for possessions, making sure you've left nothing behind at the put-in and take-out.

Occasionally a boat will come off a trailer during transportation, not having been securely fastened. This can do extensive hull damage. There's a vehicle or two that end up submerged in the river, too, usually due to faulty parking brakes on a steep ramp. This is a real shocker to the owner! I lost a truck once on a duck hunt, before a winter's dawn brightened the sky. The river had flooded earlier in the winter and gone back down. The ramp was solid ice but covered with enough dirt and debris that you couldn't tell it was ice in the darkness. While we were unloading the boat, the truck started sliding out into the river and sunk out of sight. Not a good start to a January duck hunt!

Attention should be paid to all aspects of loading and unloading. That is where most equipment is lost. Having your name, address, and phone number on every single piece of equipment will help in regaining some lost gear.

DRIFT BOATS

There are enough makes of drift boat on the market these days to fit most desires. Get all the brochures, look at as many as you can, try rowing some demos when possible, and find the features you want. Most come complete with seats, storage, front knee brace (rear ones may come as standard or optional equipment), anchor system, and trailer. They may or may not include oars (different people like different oar types) and a cover. These often cost extra. Oars cost around one hundred dollars each. Fitted boat covers go for one hundred to two hundred and fifty dollars.

Few modifications should be necessary to a well-appointed drift boat. There are some that could be needed, however, on certain makes and on some older used models. Sometimes the oar-lock position is too low. The oar handles will occasionally hit the rower's knees when he is rowing, particularly if an angler is leaning to one side or the other and isn't staying to center. This dilemma makes rowing difficult, but a surprising number of boats I've rowed have this fault. In this case, the oar-lock housing, usually wood or hard nylon blocks, can be rebuilt and raised a few inches. It would be well worth your while to do so. On the other hand, if the oar-lock position seems so high that you have to reach up too much while making oar strokes, add a seat cushion to raise the rower's position.

Foot braces matched to your height and leg length are important—much of your rowing power comes from your legs. If foot braces are absent or not ideally located, it is highly recommended to rig them up to fit you perfectly.

Nonslip traction is important for standing fishermen. Most boats now come with rough-textured floors under the knee brace position. These can wear smooth, though. Add traction strips whenever slipping starts to become a problem. It's not unusual for anglers to slip and fall out of the back of the boat. It happens every so often and could be dangerous on trickier stretches of water. An older angler slipped, fell, and hit his head on the gunwale before falling in the river and drowning last year in our neighborhood. This accident demonstrates that unexpected tragedies can occur in float-fishing. The right boat and proper rigging help prevent such disasters.

Some rowers like to add a backrest to their seat position, because this is generally nonexistent. Theoretically this interferes with rowing a bit, but guides who spend many days and long hours on stream find the added back support desirable.

Rod holders of some sort are desirable. Most are rigged just under the gunwales on the inside of the boat using Velcro, hooks of some kind, or a PVC tube.

More drift boat models are being designed for fly fishing these days. Many traditional West Coast drifters were designed to have two spin, plug, or bait anglers fish from the front seat, while back trolling with no one in the back. You'll see some with two front-seat backrests. Some 14-foot or shorter models have no back seat at all. Even though I'd much rather row one angler than two any day, note how the seats are rigged on boats you're considering. Those geared for fly fishing should have front and rear seat positions with knee braces. There should be low line-tangle potential in the design. Watch for rough edges or bolts on older boats that could tear waders. Consider side height in terms of performance needed and wind resistance. Length, width, and weight vary, too. These could be important to those wishing to float small or rampless rivers.

One modification I made to my drift boat trailer was to build a motorcycle ramp on the front for doing my own shuttles. This calls for a longer tongue, built-in hinged loading ramp, and tie-down positions. The axle position might need to be changed on some trailers so that you can still lift the tongue with ease. A wheel-fitted rolling tongue-lifter makes it possible to hitch up your boat with a light cycle on it. I had mine built with a cycle rack from the start, so balance wasn't a problem. Obviously, very light motorcycles are preferred, from mopeds to trail bikes of the smallest sizes. These provide inexpensive self-shuttling options, saving shuttle fees and allowing any hour of operation. There are places where no shuttles are readily available. Rain, snow, and dense riverside hatches make cycle shuttles less than amusing at times, so bring a helmet with a face shield! I try to shuttle in the mornings, at the beginning of the trip, to get it over with and try to avoid major bug hatches. You never know what evening weather will bring, and the bugs are sure to be thicker then.

A boat cover is a good investment and a must for a wooden boat. Covers protect finishes and color while also keeping water from collecting in the bottom of your boat. Although drift boats do have drain plugs (don't forget to put them back in!), it's added work to have to drain a boat before use. It can be almost impossible to lift the tongue to tilt and drain it if it is very full of water. Most drift boat trailers are built to tilt, allowing boats to drain. Water sitting in the bottom of a boat can discolor it and age oars and life jackets left there. A cover may keep the casual thief from walking off with your accessories, too. Most hitches lock, making it difficult for someone to hitch up your boat and drive off with it.

One other little accessory that is handy in some situations is an oar holder. This is nothing more than a 2-foot piece of PVC pipe that slides over the handle end of one oar. It should not be much wider than the diameter of the oar. When you stop to drag a boat over a gravel bar on a shallow river (which is something I do a lot of) or just tie on a fly, the tube is slid over both oar handles. This keeps them parallel and lifted up out of the water. It's particularly practical with pin and clip oar arrangements when the rower wants to jump in and out of the boat. In other cases you can just let your oars trail in the water or pull them in and across the boat. You can paint the PVC tube to match your boat if you like, which looks better than the plumbing motif.

No matter what kind of boat you choose, attention to detail will add to your enjoyment. There are boats on the market that row better than others, handle big water or wind better than others, or have better or more storage. Some knee braces and adjustable seats are more comfortable, some oars feel better in the water. Shop around and try to row as many varieties of boat as you can before investing in one. You're likely to find one that fits your style, your river, and your local float-fishing needs.

7

EXPEDITION RIGGING: GEARING UP
FOR A MULTIDAY FLOAT TRIP

A little experience with day floats on scenic western water-
ways usually leads to an interest in multiday camping expeditions.
Many famous trout and steelhead rivers offer the possibility of
overnight trips. Some are permit rivers requiring advance planning
with federal or state agencies. Other, less famous rivers can be float-
camped, too, which adds another level of adventure and relaxation
(some state's laws are more tolerant than others when it comes to
river-corridor use). There's little to match the enjoyment of camping
on the edge of a beautiful mountain river, watching the sunset, hitting
the evening hatches, then eating a hearty camp meal with a good bottle of wine. Evenings, nights, and dawns are intriguing times to be on
stream, rather than worrying about making it to the take-out and on
down the road.

Overnight trips and extended expeditions usually require a boat
of at least 14 feet in length for two or more people (a solo boater
could get by with a 12-foot or even smaller boat). Rafts handle big
loads better than drift boats and draw less water. A heavily loaded
drift boat can draw over a foot of water, taking some hard-hitting hull
abuse on shallow rocky rivers. Self-bailing rafts are the best all-
around choice if you see many overnighters in your floating future.

A 14–16-foot boat allows plenty of camping luxuries. This ain't
no backpacking trip! Thoughtful planning can include comforts while
covering the necessities plus emergency supplies. Having spent the

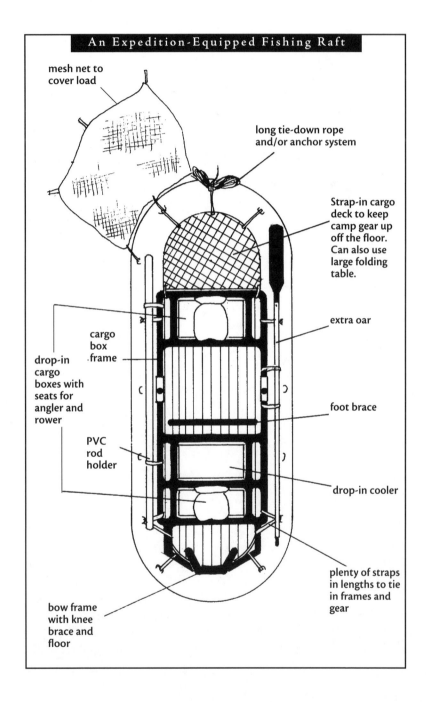

An Expedition-Equipped Fishing Raft

mesh net to cover load

long tie-down rope and/or anchor system

Strap-in cargo deck to keep camp gear up off the floor. Can also use large folding table.

extra oar

cargo box frame

drop-in cargo boxes with seats for angler and rower

foot brace

PVC rod holder

drop-in cooler

plenty of straps in lengths to tie in frames and gear

bow frame with knee brace and floor

Big tarps, held up by trees, oars, and serious staking, are the heart of many river camps.

last twenty years doing three-to-seven-day campout trips on Montana's Smith River has allowed me to get in tune with expedition packing and cooking. Both take plenty of forethought to do well. At the end of this chapter are checklists that you can use to help plan your own expeditions. The following provides an overview of one outfitter's camp set-up.

Big tarps are very handy. They are the heart of our camps. We use extrastrong custom-made ones of about 20 by 20 feet. Smaller ones will do for camps of two to six people. Days and nights of rain (or snow) are no fun without a big tarp. Cooking and standing around in the rain or in a small tent gets old after a while! Another option some outfitters use is a large wall tent. This is a bulkier and more elaborate set-up.

Big tarps give protection from both rain and sun. This is important on those blistering summer-heat-wave trips. They keep campers and food coolers shaded, prolonging the life of ice and fresh foods. Tarps are also used to cover the boat's load. They can be folded to shape and placed over a load before netting or tying down. (The camp load on a raft is usually confined to the back half, which leaves the front half for anglers. One big tarp can cover all the gear.) This protects your equipment from rain during the floating day and can lessen the need for so many costly waterproof bags where big white water isn't an issue.

The biggest problem with tarps is wind-related. Our fierce Montana winds can destroy all but the best-set camps from time to time. Wind will rip the grommets out of cheap tarps (you can then tie knots in the corners or use the old "rock wrapped in the tarp" tie-down method). Stakes will come flying out of the ground in a big or sudden blow. The best stakes we've come up with are 2–3-foot sections of conduit. These can be driven into most kinds of ground and gravel with a big hammer or axe butt. They can also be taken back out easily enough. They hold very well when deeply sunk and properly angled and last a long time. Those cheap plastic and small wood or iron stakes aren't worth a hoot when it comes to tarping. Don't cut green wood off trees, either. This is now looked down upon along our heavily used river corridors. Firewood becomes scarce and people hack green trees for no good reason. Campsites can become rather shabby looking. If you do need a fire or stake wood (where it's legal), look for it at midday when floating between camps, not at them. It's much easier to find that way.

We always stake out tarps in readiness for the biggest storms at each camp, using trees as tie-downs whenever possible. The long conduit stakes work well on treeless tarp corners, and we use long ropes and oars to keep the tarp at our desired "walk under" height. Ropes of at least 30 feet should be attached to each corner, with four extra ones on hand to reinforce the side midpoints. Sometimes we double-stake corners if the ground is soft or the position seems shaky. Ropes are set along the sides to tighten the tarp like a drum. It's much better to be overstaked than understaked when that big thunderstorm hits! Sudden gusts of 60 mph are not uncommon. I hate to have prepared a complex dinner, then have the tarp blow away, knocking down the entire kitchen and dumping the food in the dirt!

We as guides usually sleep under the tarp on cots or on the ground. Our guests stay in tents that are far enough away so as not to hear us snore (or vice versa). Though even the best-laid tarp has blown away on occasion and even collapsed under the weight of heavy nighttime snow (a rude awakening!), for the most part tarps have given us decades of sun, cooking, and sleeping shelter.

Any design of tent can be brought along to match your personality and the size of your boat. There are plenty of choices, from the smallest, lightest backpacking models to roomy 12-by-12 or larger models that you can stand up and even cook in. Your choice in float-and-camp gear can reflect how much comfort you desire versus how much time you want to spend hauling it around, setting it up, and tearing it down. The young often prefer strip-down lightweight camps, which also cost less. Many older floaters have come to appreciate the comforts of a table and chair, a tent you can stand up to enter, and a well-padded cot!

In spring and fall, when the potential for cold mornings and evenings is high, big tents make good cookhouses and dining areas. Stoves and lanterns heat a tent quickly, giving it a homey ambience. Cold wind, which otherwise sucks the heat right out of a meal, is blocked, along with rain, bugs, or snow. You must have some ventilation, though, to allow fumes to disperse. Such large tents need to be securely staked out, too, and even roped down. I've seen one blow across a meadow with one very surprised lady still inside!

Chairs and tables are great comforts when one is spending days on the river. Whittling at a steak with a paper plate on your lap while sitting on the ground just doesn't do it! There are plenty of portable collapsing models around to choose from.

For cooking and preparing food, sturdier tables are desirable, ones built to working height so you don't have to bend over to slice and dice. These are available from specialty river equipment dealers and catalogs, generally in the white-water market. They're rather pricey but worthwhile on stream if many riverside days are in your future. You could build one yourself, as river bums are apt to do. They can be designed to fit across the back of your raft as a loading platform for camp gear, and thus must be sturdily constructed.

There are plenty of waterproof bag and box options around these days to carry dry goods and duffel. Traditionally, white-water enthusiasts required totally waterproof containers in case of flips. Some of these were expensive or heavy. Most fishing floaters don't expect to flip or get drenched by big waves, though. They can get by

This ain't backpacking! River camps allow more luxuries, comforts, and fancier meals.

with the larger household storage containers sold in discount stores, and with the waterproof bags now found in most outdoor-product catalogs. Specialty river equipment catalogs will fill you in on the best, most rugged, and higher tech gear. Tie in or net over your gear securely when floating, though, to keep from losing it overboard during collisions with boulders and such. Nothing of value should be able to wash free, even in a flip. Ultimately, everything should be tied, strapped, or netted down.

Some permit rivers have special regulations. Fires may not be permitted, or you may be required to take a fire plan. In extreme cases (like the Grand Canyon, which does have some big trout!) you even have to pack out all human waste. We're talking fecal matter here. In such cases special equipment can be required by the permitting agency and will be inspected by them at the put-in site.

Cooking on the river varies from the most basic to gourmet fare. Just about anything can be made with the right planning, equipment, and perhaps a little advance preparation at home. It's just about as easy to prepare some great dishes as it is simple ones. River folk always appreciate that extra effort, especially at mealtime! Everything does seem to taste better riverside after a long day of fishing.

On longer expeditions, taking care of your coolers, food, and ice becomes a concern. There are tricks of the trade that help, and foods that last longer than others. Plenty of block ice, two to three blocks per large cooler, kept stacked together, should last up to seven days. It will only last this long if people aren't continually opening and closing the cooler, though, and if it's babied through the trip. Meats, juices, bread, and such for the later days of the trip should be frozen beforehand to prolong their cooler life. (On cool-weather trips this won't be necessary. You might even have trouble defrosting them.)

Keep coolers out of direct sunlight at all times. Cover them when they are in the boat, and put them in the shade of a tarp as soon as you reach camp. This is the first thing I do after setting up a tarp. Rotting food isn't much fun. As the sun crosses the sky and the tarp shadow moves, relocate coolers to keep them shaded.

We have one trick that really helps stretch ice life to seven or more days. We soak large, thick white beach or bath towels with water and cover each cooler with them. They are rewetted in the river whenever they even begin to dry. Thick white towels hold moisture a long time and act like an air conditioner. You can feel an appreciable difference between the air temperature and other items in your boat compared to the wetted cooler. I'd guess there's a 20–30-degree difference. We keep wet towels on coolers in the shade of the tarp, too, every moment of the day. This adds one to three days of life to ice, making a major difference in the preservation of fresh foods during hot-weather trips.

When loading coolers at the start, we'll pack the block ice on the cooler bottoms bunched together. Frozen foods go in next, along with other stuff that won't crush. Lighter and fragile items go on top. In coolers other than those with fresh fragile produce we spread cube ice over the tops to fill in gaps. Such a cooler kept covered with a wet towel and seldom opened will hold ice a long time.

Some outfitters on very long trips will have coolers packed for day-by-day use. They'll even duct-tape coolers closed to seal out hot summer air. We usually categorize coolers by meat, dairy, vegetable and fruit, and drink. In this way meat blood is kept out of cheese, fresh fruits and vegetables aren't crushed and spoiled by heavy objects and too much ice contact, and coolers that people open and close the most—drink coolers—aren't compromising meats and other foods because their ice is melting.

Making sure everything, including canned drinks, is well chilled before going into coolers helps immensely, too. Adding cans of drinks at room temperature to ice immediately begins to melt it. Proper attention to these details will enable you to make ice last throughout your trip. We sometimes take an ice cooler filled with nothing but block and cube ice, especially if the crew is fond of cocktails on ice come evening. For extralong expeditions dry ice can be added atop an ice cooler and it can be taped shut.

There are foods that last better than others. For instance, strawberries tend to mold after a couple days. Leaking fish will really funk out a cooler if not perfectly wrapped. Tomatoes are likely to get smashed if you don't constantly relocate them to the top of the cooler after digging around for other foods. Fragile and quick-spoiling items should be planned for use early in the trip. Longer-lasting things like frozen meat, celery, and potatoes can be saved for the last days. Some fruits and vegetables don't need to be kept on ice at all. They can be kept in a dry box in the shade or covered with a wet towel. Potatoes, onions, cantaloupe, apples, and oranges are examples.

Of course, you could dispense with fresh foods altogether and just take canned and prepackaged stuff, and a few hunks of meat, pasta, and rice. There are better canned alternatives these days, with better spicing and less sugar and salt. Many dry packaged goods have become tastier, too. Freeze-dried backpacking meals are always out there, though they don't seem overpopular with floaters. Cooking alternatives are plentiful.

We favor propane kitchens using several two- to three-burner stoves and lanterns. There are also oven and barbecue-grill propane accessories. A large propane tank will give us a good week of steady use.

Some floaters are into Dutch oven cooking, which opens up many baking possibilities, including cakes, casseroles, muffins, and the like. These are fueled by charcoal briquettes. Light-load trippers might prefer one-burner backpacking or two-burner fuel stoves. This will depend on your temperament, party size, length of trip, and preference, or lack thereof, for good food. Many guide operations and private floaters delve deep into the gourmet world on river trips. The surprise of outstanding meals and fine wines heightens the overall trip experience. To others, hot dogs, baked beans, and beer represent the true camping experience. As long as I get full at the end of a long rowing day I'm happy!

The following checklists are taken from the years of guiding I've done with Montana River Outfitters. These could be more extensive than you might want, but most options are covered. We usually end up with a four- to six-page checklist for our guided expeditions on Montana's Smith, South Fork of the Flathead, and other regional rivers. You can photocopy and edit these to meet your floating needs.

Float-Fishing Checklists

DRIFT BOAT AND PRAM DAY-TRIP LIST

- anchor and rope
- boat and trailer
- boat cover
- boat net
- camera and video
- check light hookups
- cooler with ice
- drain plugs
- drinks
- extra clothes for all weather conditions
- extra keys
- extra water
- first-aid kit
- fishing license
- flashlight
- flies
- food
- guidebooks
- hat
- insect repellent
- life jackets
- lunch storage box
- lunch utensils
- maps
- oar locks
- oars
- oar tube
- personal duffel
- raingear
- rods and reels
- rowing gloves
- seat cushions
- shuttle arrangements
- stove and fuel
- sunglasses
- sunscreen and lip balm
- tackle
- throw rope
- waders
- waterproof bags
- waterproof camera box
- other:

RAFT SUPPLEMENT

cargo deck and netting
drop-in boxes
patch kit
pumps (electric and manual)
raft
rod holder
rowing frame(s)
seats
straps and tie-downs
other:

OVERNIGHT-TRIP SUPPLEMENT

axe (can be used as hammer for
    stakes)
big tarp with ropes attached and
    4–8 stakes
biodegradable soap
buckets
cameras and film
candles
cargo decks and nets
chairs
charcoal
clothes for all weather conditions
coolers
cots
dining table
dishwashing supplies
dry goods boxes
Dutch oven
emergency radio
expanded first-aid kit
extra keys
extra rods
extra straps and tie-downs
50-foot rope (to tie up boats
    at night and for wraps)
fire starter
fishing gear
flashlights
fly-tying kit
food and drink
garbage bags
grill for pit cooking
ice
insect repellent
kitchen box
lantern and mantles
lighter fluid
matches and lighters
menu
mirror
pads and mattresses
paper cups
personal medications
personal toilet kit
personal washing bowl
pillow
portable toilet
propane barbecue grill
propane hookups
propane oven
propane tanks
raingear
saw
shovel
shuttle arrangements
skin cream
sleeping bags
solar shower
stoves and fuel
sunscreen
tablecloth
tables for stove and kitchen
tents and stakes
thermos
toilet paper
tools and extra propane hoses
video camera
water containers
water filter
waterproof bags
waterproof boxes
white towels
other:

KITCHEN BOX EQUIPMENT

aluminum foil
bleach
bottle opener
bowls
can opener
carafe and thermos
chef knives
coffee cups
coffeepot
coffee, teas
cooking oils
condiments
corkscrew
creamer
cutting boards
dish draining rack
dish rags and towels
dish soap (biodegradable)
dish tub
drinking glasses
Dutch oven
flashlight
frying pans
garbage bags
grater
griddle
hot chocolate
hot pads
kitchen first-aid kit
ladle
large fork
large mixing bowls
large soup pot
marinades
matches and lighter
menu
napkins
paper cups
paper towels
pitcher
plates
salt and pepper
saucepans
scrubber
self-sealing plastic bags
serving platter
serving spoons
sharpening steel
shish kebab sticks
silverware
spatulas
spices
steak knives
steamer
sugar and sugar substitute
syrup and jellies
tablecloth
tongs
tools for propane and camp work
toothpicks
vegetable peeler
water filter with tablets
other:

BASIC EXTENDED-TRIP SHOPPING LIST

STAPLES

aluminum foil
baking powder
bleach
boxed meals (i.e., macaroni and
    cheese)
canned foods
cereals
chocolate bars
cookies
cooking chocolate
cooking oils
corn chips
corn starch
crackers
dish soap
dried fruit
flour
garbage bags

STAPLES (CONT.)

honey
jellies
ketchup
marinades
matches
mayonnaise
mustards
pancake mix
paper towels
pasta
pickles
potato chips
pretzels

rice
salad dressings
salsa
salt and pepper
sauce and gravy mixes
self-sealing plastic bags
spices for menu
sugar and sugar substitute
syrups
Tabasco
toilet paper
other:

DRINKS

beer
bottled waters
coffee and teas
hot chocolate
juices
liquors (drinking and cooking)

milk
powdered drink mix
sodas
wine
other:

MEATS

BREAKFAST MEATS
bacon
Canadian bacon
ham
sausage
steaks
other:
LUNCHMEATS
corned beef
fried chicken
ham
pastrami
roast beef
salami

smoked turkey
turkey
other:
DINNER MEATS
chicken
Cornish game hens
fish
lamb
pork chops and loins
shish kebab beef
shrimp
steaks
other:

VEGETABLES

asparagus
broccoli
carrots
cauliflower
celery
corn
cucumber
garlic
green peppers
hash browns
herbs

hot peppers
lettuce
onions
potatoes
red peppers
shallots
snow peas
spinach
tomatoes
other:

FRUIT

apples
avocado
bananas
berries
canned fruit
cantaloupe
frozen fruit
grapes
lemon

limes
melon
oranges
pears
pineapple
plums
strawberries
other:

DAIRY

butter
cream
cream cheese
eggs and/or egg substitute

margarine
milks
sour cream
whipped cream

CHEESES

blue
Cheddar
jack

Parmesan
Swiss
other:

Breads

bagels
cakes
cheese rolls
cookies
croissants
dinner rolls
English muffins
fajita shells
French bread

kaiser rolls
onion rolls
pies
pita bread
poor boys
pound cake
sandwich bread
other:

Etc.

charcoal
first-aid supplies
fishing licenses
flies
fuel for vehicles
ice

lantern mantles
lighter fluid
propane
shuttle and permit fees
stove fuel
other:

It's not unusual to have one or more people on a trip who only eat low-fat foods, are vegetarians, or are allergic to certain foods. Some are on medications, are allergic to bee stings, have heart condi-

River trips make great family adventures and help interest kids in outdoor experiences.

tions, or what have you. It helps to be aware of these things in advance on longer expeditions.

Although preparing for a long expedition is a major chore in itself and one not to be underestimated, the comforts on-stream make good planning worthwhile. If all share evenly in the planning, loading, rowing, camp set-up, cooking, dishwashing, camp break-down, shuttling, trip unloading, and equipment clean-up, things will go quickly and smoothly. Those who stand around while others do the work or who don't show up to load and unload tend not to be asked on future expeditions! Making sure there's no clash of personalities at the onset helps insure enjoyable trips, too. These are no small matters. Eventually, small cadres of voyagers tend to click. Many travel together over decades down North America's or the world's best rivers and fisheries. It would take more than a lifetime to experience them all. I know many a river addict, old and young.

8

TRAILERING, RAMP USE, AND RIVER ETIQUETTE

*T*o those who spend a lot of time on rivers and boat ramps, the unwritten rules of the game become a code to operate by. The inexperienced sometimes don't have a clue as to why others might be irritated with them. There are proper ways to do things in keeping harmony on the river.

Life at a boat ramp these days isn't quite as pleasant as it was twenty years ago, when no one else was likely to be around. There can be regular traffic jams at popular boat ramps now. Unloading and loading procedures should be streamlined to speed up ramp use. The following are some hints on keeping ramp tension down.

First, load and unload quickly, then get your vehicle out of the way. Don't park on the ramp drinking coffee and tying on flies if others are waiting to use it. If you are in line waiting to use the ramp, use that time to load your fishing gear into the boat and untie it (except for the winch tie-down at the bow) so that when your turn comes you can quickly push your boat off the trailer into the river and pull the vehicle away. It is particularly irritating to wait on those who choose to inflate and rig or deflate a raft on the ramp itself, instead of doing this off to one side and then using the ramp when the raft is rigged. Some unthinking people also park in such a fashion as to block the approach to the ramp, not taking into consideration how much space a trailering vehicle needs to operate.

After getting your boat in the water, move it away from the ramp itself. Tie it up or anchor it where it's not in any other boat's

Showing courtesy to wading anglers and other floaters is a daily practice on our well-used western rivers. These float fishers are floating behind the waders so as not to disrupt their fishing or scare their fish.

way. Don't park it right next to someone else's boat, where it's going to repeatedly bump into it. Treat other people's boats like gold. New- and wooden-boat owners are likely to be hostile to someone who mindlessly slams a boat into theirs. Some unthinking floaters with older craft will let their boats frequently bump against others at launch sites. You wouldn't do it with your car, so don't do it with your boat! Try to park it well away from others, pull it up on the bank, or have someone hold it in place so currents and wind don't slam it into another craft. If you go off for a long shuttle and leave your boat in the river, park well away from the ramp. Have someone stay with the boat in case it needs to be moved or held in place. This also helps avert theft, which is all too common these days, even along backcountry rivers. I've also seen unattended parked boats get blown away by strong winds.

When loading back up at the end of the day, get your boat on the trailer, then quickly pull the vehicle away. Don't sit there blocking the ramp while unrigging rods, taking off waders, and drinking a beer. Streamlining and minimizing your ramp-use time makes the floating day more enjoyable for everyone: Remember that some people might have to drive a couple hundred miles after getting off the river. A parade of slothlike floater take-outs naturally irritates those who have to get somewhere and don't want to fall asleep at the wheel along the way. Long days on the river make you more tired than usual. Watch out for deer!

When floating, give wade fishers a wide berth. Leave them plenty of extra water to fish by not casting into it. This helps create the illusion that they have some water to fish that hasn't already been flogged by a parade of boats on busier days. To a wading angler, boats look closer than floaters realize. If the other side of the river is unoccupied, row over there as soon as a wade fisher comes into view. Resist the urge to make one more cast to a hot spot just upstream from him.

Space yourself evenly from other boats. Slow down to fall farther behind. If you're ahead, float a little faster for a while to put some space between you and a boat that's right behind you. Don't get into racing matches to be first to hot spots. If you're going to do that, why not just get a big power boat and rip the river up getting there? While you're at it, take a seine net and get all the fish! There seem to be a lot of people, including some guides, on the river these days who would be better off on a tennis court or playing some other urban and concrete-based competition sport. Go with the flow, fish where you are, forget the rest of humanity, and enjoy the day. That's what a day on the river is for.

Negotiating Ramps

Watching a novice back a trailer down a tight ramp is always amusing, unless you're in a hurry to get on or off the river and are right behind him! He'll not likely grasp the basic trailering concept without experience or instruction.

Backing is the trickiest part of trailering. It feels unnatural on the first attempts. To turn the trailer one way when backing, you have to turn the vehicle the opposite way. When, or actually just before, the trailer has turned enough, straighten the vehicle to push the trailer backward. Because most drift boat trailers have short wheelbases and tongues, they turn quickly—perhaps a little too quickly for a beginner—for they seem to want to turn one way or the other even when you don't want them to. Indeed, going straight back and keeping the trailer backing in a straight line is the hardest thing to do. Only experience with a particular rig and trailer will give you the necessary feel for the job. It's easier to learn on big spacious ramps rather than narrow, steep, angled ones!

Practice using your mirrors right from the start to follow your trailer's backward progress. This is much easier than straining your neck to look over your shoulders. You'll want mirrors on both sides of your vehicle. When the trailer begins turning even a little too much to one side, immediately correct by turning the vehicle in the opposite direction. Don't allow the trailer to get way off track or jackknife, because this can damage the trailer or vehicle. Slow and easy is the way to learn. You'll be more likely to oversteer than anything, and to let the trailer turn too far off-course before correcting its path. In a tight situation you can unhitch the trailer and manually align it with the ramp as long as the ground is level. Rehitch it before heading down a steep ramp! Some people put a hitch on their front bumper. Hooking the boat there makes it easier to maneuver down difficult ramps.

It's easy enough to see your boat and trailer when you are backing at the put-in. A boatless trailer at the take-out (and possibly in the dark) is another matter. It can be impossible to see a narrow, boatless trailer when backing with a tall vehicle such as a Suburban, which blocks your low view. The trailer only comes into sight when it's swinging to one side, which at times means it's turned farther than you want it to be. With a pickup truck you can drop the tailgate to see the trailer, but this isn't always an option with some other vehicles.

There are ways to work around this. For starters, you can have a boatmate behind your vehicle giving hand signals and possibly using a flashlight to point and illuminate the way. You could also attach tall wands (with or without small flags) to the outside edges of your trailer near the back end. These should be tall enough and angled outwards so as to be seen in your mirrors when you are backing straight. They can be permanent or removable. It helps to have widely placed mirrors on both sides of your vehicle, such as those used by RVers.

This provides a little more mirror angle to help you see behind your rig.

When you buy a trailer, try to get one that's wide enough to see out both mirrors when car and trailer are aligned. This will make it easier for you to see as you back, and you can also see both trailer tires when you are driving in order to check for flat tires or burned-up bearings (a wobbling wheel). Backing your hubs in and out of water can ruin them quickly if you don't stay on top of the regreasing game. I try not to get my trailer axle hubs in the water at all.

My trailer is a little wider and longer than average, because I have a motorcycle rack built on the tongue. I can see the trailer in both mirrors when it is straight, and it backs well, having a longer wheelbase. It's a little tougher to back down very angled, twisty ramps, but that is rarely a problem in my case. I like being able to see both trailer tires when I drive.

When heading down the road with a trailer you'll need to take corners a little wider than usual. Watch the trailer's cornering progress in the mirror. Soon you'll get over jumping curbs with the trailer tire, scraping your boat on ramp-edge bushes, or possibly doing more serious damage to it. Most drift boat trailers are short enough to follow a vehicle well; you can drive in a near-normal cornering fashion.

Backing trailers takes the ability to conceptualize and lots of practice to master, kind of like rowing. It's just one more skill that will grow out of your float-fishing experiences.

When floating rivers, be aware of the different states' trespass regulations. Some states allow access to the bank and streambed below the high-water mark. In other states, the landowner owns the banks and streambed, and even anchoring is technically illegal. Future floating rights could depend on how well today's float anglers observe (or change) current laws. Though it shouldn't have to be mentioned, don't trespass or litter on-stream. Pick up other people's litter when it's convenient and take it out in your boat. When everybody does a little to clean up the river environment the results start showing in short order. Courtesy, respect for landowner rights, giving wade fishers plenty of room, and spacing evenly from other fishing boats are all daily etiquette requirements when float-fishing rivers.

CONCLUSION

*R*ivers are among our greatest natural resources and are home to myriad fish, game, and migratory bird species. Their recreational importance is great but hard to put a dollar figure on. Noting humankind's tendency to ruin everything in its path through overpopulation, overdevelopment, and underplanning, it's important to protect and improve river habitats now by joining local conservation efforts and national groups like American Rivers and Trout Unlimited.

It's also important to resist the urge to have your own riverside cabin and thus help destroy the resource you love. Subdivisions along rivers add no beauty, and subdivision growth eventually dooms the area to scenic and game-resource mediocrity. For with subdivision comes the desire for flood management, then channelization, waste pollution, asphalt and fertilizer runoff, and loss of protective riparian zones and game habitat. Rivers and their immediate corridors do best when they are left alone!

There is little that can match the beauty and richness of natural rivers in uncompromised settings. The hypnotizing effect of moving water—ripples, eddies, and glides—of the rings of rising trout and banter of migrating waterfowl has an undeniable appeal to the human psyche, which otherwise seems to get lost in caffeinated, nonstop urban growth. The feel of oars in your hands, the push of clean flowing water, and the sight of wild landscapes sweeping by should be a right and a national priority, not a pastime doomed by needless suburban sprawl and new shopping malls.

But as long as water flows and trout rise, they will mesmerize floaters like myself, whose fishy tunnel vision leads us to rivers near and far. Our timetables will be set by things as unlikely as cfs readings, aquatic insect hatches, the habits of fishes, and the color of leaves on trees. We'll try to dream the rest of the world away for that one big rising brown trout today!

APPENDIX: HATCHES AND FLY PATTERNS FOR FLY FISHING WESTERN RIVERS

*I*t's always of benefit for the rower and angler to know something of the aquatic insects that hatch from a chosen river, and to have some flies on hand that are most likely to fool fish. Hatches and fly patterns have filled many volumes of books. It's a complex subject that's too complicated to cover completely here. Nonetheless, a basic understanding will go a long way toward improving your catch. Rivers, hatches, and trout vary, though. A little research ahead of time will help define for you the hatches, times, and fly patterns you need for a particular place and time. Check with local fishing shops for updated information.

We won't get bogged down in too much Latin or nitpick over fine details. This information is presented with the beginner in mind; advanced anglers will already know most of this. Insatiable angler-entomologists will dig through more advanced texts.

Let's take a generalized look at hatches and trout food through the season.

General Western Hatches

Hatch	Color	Hook #	Common fly patterns	Notes
Midges	gray-black	#18–24	Griffith's Gnat, Midge pupae, Brassie	Will bring some trout to surface in winter in slow eddies and flats.
Little winter stoneflies	black	#18–14	none, can use black caddis	Numerous on swifter rivers; sunny days bring best hatches.
Other year-round foods: sculpins, minnows, crayfish, worms, nymphs in general	black, brown, olive, grays, red	#2–14	Woolly Bugger, Muddler Minnow, Zonker, crayfish, San Juan Worm, weighted nymphs	Large wet flies will usually catch some fish, including big ones. Weighted nymphs are always a good bet.
Midges	gray-black, olive-tan	#18–24	as above	As above, can be mixed with mayflies and caddis.
Spring stoneflies	gray, black, olive-brown	#16–8	black caddis, Stimulator, stonefly nymphs	Sunny days often best; can be mixed with mayflies. Some good fish will rise before runoff starts.
Little blue-winged olives (*Baetis* mayflies)	olive-gray, gray wings	#16–20	Parachute Adams, Sparkle Dun, Olive Thorax, Pheasant Tail Nymph, Bead-head P.T.	Excellent afternoon hatch. Best on overcast, damp days. Trout like this hatch!
Western march brown mayfly	olive-brown, gray mottled wings	#14–16	March Brown, Parachute Adams (olive-brown body), Comparadun, Gray Wulff	Good late-morning, early-afternoon hatch on swifter rivers. Can be mixed with olive mayflies, midges, and spring stoneflies
Caddis	grays, browns, olive bodies, too	#14–18	Elkhair Caddis, Henryville Caddis, Missouri River Special, Sparkle Pupa, Beadhead Caddis worms, soft-hackles	Some April-to-May caddis hatches are very profuse. Emergers can be more important than drys at times.
Large stonefly nymphs	black, dark brown, tan	#4–8	Woolly Bugger, Bitch Creek, Montana Nymph, Kaufmann's Stone, Golden Stone	As rivers rise in May and June, large stonefly nymphs become prominent in many a swift-water trout's diet.

WINTER—DECEMBER TO FEBRUARY

SPRING—MARCH TO MAY

Hatch	Color	Hook #	Common fly patterns	Notes
Little blue-winged olives	olive-gray, gray wings	#16–24	as above	BWOs continue into summer. Can be smaller now, down to #24. Best on cool, rainy days.
Pale morning dun mayflies	yellowish with pale green hues	#16–22	PMD Sparkle Dun, various PMD dry flies and emergers	Prominent western hatch from late June into August. Trout can get very picky on this hatch! Can hatch mid- to late morning or evening.
Green and brown drake mayflies	deep olive brown and dark brown with mottled wings	#10–12	Para-Drakes, Green Drake, Green Drake emergers, Brown Drake, Brown Drake emergers	These big mayflies hatch in late June and early July in most places, often in high water conditions, but can be found as late as August and even September at the highest elevations. This is true of many hatches. Green drakes hatch late mornings into early afternoons, brown drakes hatch late afternoons and evenings.
Salmon fly	dark gray top and wings, orange hues on abdomen	#2–6	Stimulator, big black stonefly nymphs	The largest aquatic insect! Hatches in high-water flows. Hit or miss type fishing. Timing the hatch is very important but still doesn't guarantee success. Found from mid-May to mid-July depending on altitude and locale.
Golden stonefly	mottled brownish tan	#6–8	Golden Stone drys and nymphs	Hatches just after the larger salmon fly, when waters are likely to be clearing. This hatch lasts longer than the salmon flies and can provide better fishing.

SUMMER—JUNE TO MID-SEPTEMBER

Hatch	Color	Hook #	Common fly patterns	Notes
Caddis and microcaddis	browns, grays, black, tan	#14–22	Elkhair and Feather-Wing Caddis drys, Sparkle Pupa, soft-hackle	Many species of caddis hatch over the summer months and into fall. Some are very small, requiring tiny, precise imitations. Pupae often work better than drys.
Trico mayfly spinners	black and olive with clear wings and long tails	#18–24	Parachute Trico, Trico spinner	A very dense morning hatch and spinner fall. There can be so many tiny bugs in the air that they look like fog! Brings up large numbers of picky rising trout from early July to late September.
Little yellow, green, and brown stoneflies	bright yellows, greens, tans, some with red abdomens	#10–16	Yellow Sallies, Stimulators, Trudes	Could be locally important when rivers drop and clear.
Other mayflies possible	grays, tan, pale yellow, brown, pink	#14–18	Parachutes, Sparkle Duns, Wulffs, spent-wings, and a variety of small to medium nymphs and emergers	Different water types can show varying hatches, even on the same river. Altitude, temperature, and streambed composition all affect species encountered.
Grasshoppers, ants, beetles	grays, browns, black	#4–10 #14–18	Dave's Hopper, Parachute Hopper, CDC Ant, flying ant, foam beetle	Land-based insects make up a good percentage of a trout's diet from midsummer to early fall. Midday hatches are sparse at this time. These bugs fill that void. Trout grow to love hoppers by late summer!

SUMMER—JUNE TO MID-SEPTEMBER

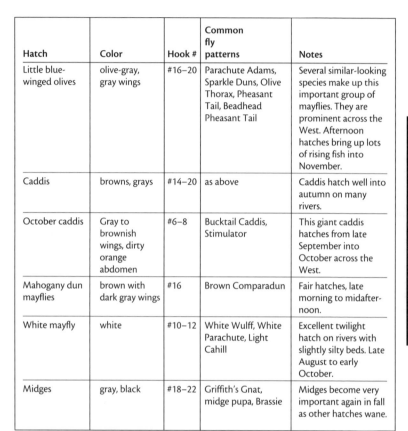

Hatch	Color	Hook #	Common fly patterns	Notes
Little blue-winged olives	olive-gray, gray wings	#16–20	Parachute Adams, Sparkle Duns, Olive Thorax, Pheasant Tail, Beadhead Pheasant Tail	Several similar-looking species make up this important group of mayflies. They are prominent across the West. Afternoon hatches bring up lots of rising fish into November.
Caddis	browns, grays	#14–20	as above	Caddis hatch well into autumn on many rivers.
October caddis	Gray to brownish wings, dirty orange abdomen	#6–8	Bucktail Caddis, Stimulator	This giant caddis hatches from late September into October across the West.
Mahogany dun mayflies	brown with dark gray wings	#16	Brown Comparadun	Fair hatches, late morning to midafternoon.
White mayfly	white	#10–12	White Wulff, White Parachute, Light Cahill	Excellent twilight hatch on rivers with slightly silty beds. Late August to early October.
Midges	gray, black	#18–22	Griffith's Gnat, midge pupa, Brassie	Midges become very important again in fall as other hatches wane.

AUTUMN—MID-SEPTEMBER THROUGH NOVEMBER

Late Winter–Early Spring (February to April)

HATCHES

There are few hatches now. Gray-black midges are numerous, bringing some trout and whitefish to the surface. Flies in #16–26 could be needed. Little black stoneflies (#16) hatch on sunnier days, larger #14–8 olive-brown stoneflies show toward the end of this period. Both can bring trout to the surface on rocky mountain rivers.

Small, #16–20, olive-gray mayflies (*Baetis*) begin hatching afternoons as early as March on some rivers, in April on others. This is one of the year's best overall hatches, continuing into May and June and reappearing in September through November. Spring insects and the trout that rise to them show a decided preference for humid overcast days. Bright sunshine shows less rising-fish action, except in the case of early-season stoneflies, which like warm sunshine. Clouds are your allies now.

A #14–16 mottled gray-brown mayfly could show up in late March or April. Elsewhere, it might not appear until May. This is the western march brown. The first caddis might show at the end of this period, too.

SUBSURFACE EMERGERS

Midge pupae in #16–24 are very important in this time period. Small, #16–20, olive-brown mayfly emergers work when mayfly hatches kick in. Larger #14–18 caddis emergers could improve catch rates when that hatch starts.

DEEP

Minnow, sculpin, crayfish, and leech patterns are always worth a try any time of year. These can be large, sizes #8–4. Size #18–14 mayfly nymphs; caddis, worm and cased; scuds; cressbugs; plus #10–6 San Juan Worms are all prime early-season producers, especially on tailwater rivers and spring creeks. Beadhead variations seem to work especially well. Tiny #18–24 midge larvae are good droppers on slow rich tailwaters. Stonefly nymphs in #10–4 are good bets in swift mountain rivers where those flies are populous. They should be weighted and fished deep.

Little black stoneflies in sizes #16–18 hatch from February into May. They can bring trout to the surface on sunny days, when they're most active. This is before mountain snows start melting, which brings rivers to annual runoff highs in May and June.

Baetis mayflies, known as little blue-winged olives, are a major spring and fall hatch across the West and elsewhere. Though small, only #16–20, their profuse numbers and tendency to ride the currents a long time make their hatches premium afternoon fishing affairs.

Western march brown mayflies favor swifter water and might be found on-stream from March to late May, depending on altitude and locale. This #14–16 fly is one of the better early-season hatches.

Beadhead nymphs are excellent producers before, during, and after a hatch. They can be dead-drifted deep between hatches and swung across the currents or fished shallow beneath a strike indicator when trout are near the surface.

Sculpins, a bottom-hugging baitfish, are always worth imitating—big fish love them.

Big, #4–8 stonefly nymphs are always good early-season bets in swift mountain rivers where the naturals dwell. This is a golden stone natural.

Spring–Early Summer (May to June)

HATCHES

At this time #18–24 midges, #16–20 olive-gray *Baetis* mayflies, #14–16 western march brown mayflies, and #14–8 dark stoneflies continue hatching. Caddis become more numerous, mostly #14–18 in dark grays, and browns. The bodies are often olive or amber to brown.

Hatches of giant salmon flies (a stonefly) take place on many mountain rivers as early as May. More are seen toward late June and into July at the highest elevations.

A plethora of hatches starts booming out in mid- to late June, including #10–12 green and brown drake mayflies, #16–18 pale morning dun (PMD) mayflies, and a variety of swift-water mayflies that are mostly in the #14–16 size range. Colors range from slate gray to olive-brown to tan. Not all rivers have all these hatches, but local inquiry should take you a long way in solving the hatch puzzle. The fishing can be so much better and more interesting during a hatch, so a little research is worthwhile. There can be such a variety of bugs hatching on mountain rivers that attractor patterns like Trudes, Wulffs, Humpies, and Stimulators in sizes #16–10 will produce well. Tailwater rivers and spring creeks usually show less diversity of insect species but great numbers of the ones there. Expect the trout here to be pickier and productive fly patterns smaller.

SUBSURFACE EMERGERS

Emergers become much more important from late June through fall. Traditional wet flies and soft-hackles in #12–18 can work well. Beadhead variations are killers. LaFontaine Sparkle Pupae become very effective.

Mayfly nymphs, caddis pupae, and midge pupae fished just beneath the surface produce best at times when trout appear to be rising but won't take dry flies. Many recent and evolving emerger patterns imitate flies that are just under or half-under half-atop the surface. These variations are especially important when fishing caddis and PMD mayfly hatches.

Caddis begin showing up as early as April on many western rivers. Some of these early hatches are very profuse.

PMD, or pale morning dun, mayflies are prominent western hatches from late June into August. Matched by size #16–22 dry flies and emergers, this late-morning and evening hatch can dominate the trouts' attention when emerging.

DEEP

Large streamers continue to work well. Brown Woolly Buggers are among my favorites. May through June is the high-water period on most Rocky Mountain rivers, and sometimes larger flies work better in muddying waters. Very dark or very bright patterns are favored by most. A lot of built-in weight might be needed to get them deep enough. Many trout will hug the banks at this time and hunker down behind riffle drop-offs.

Large #8–2 stonefly nymphs fished along the bottom and banks are the ticket where salmon flies and golden stoneflies abound. Also, #14–10 Beadhead Hare's Ears, Prince Nymphs, and the like work well, especially as swift rivers start to clear for the summer.

Tailwaters and spring creeks fish more consistently with small stuff: #16–22 mayfly, caddis, and midge larvae tend to work best. Small Beadhead variations are big producers. Popular patterns include Pheasant Tail Nymphs, Brassies, Sparkle Pupae, soft-hackles, Serendipities, cress bugs, and scuds. San Juan Worms with little nymph droppers are good bets. Don't neglect big Woolly Buggers, either. These selective fish do pounce on them from time to time.

High Summer (July to September)

HATCHES

Rivers drop and clear after May and June's high water; many hatches occur and overlap. Giant salmon flies and golden stoneflies hatch into July on famous rivers like the Yellowstone. Smaller, #10–16 brown, green, and yellow stoneflies take over as the larger species fizzle for the year. Most stoneflies will be gone by mid-August.

The larger, #10–12 green and brown drake mayflies continue into early July. Similar-sized gray drakes are found on some rivers. Swift streams can show hatches of #12–16 "pink lady" mayflies in midsummer, a light grayish–pink-hued species.

Smaller mayflies become much more important now, and #16–22 pale morning dun mayflies rank high. Trout can be very picky when feeding on them. Bring both dry flies and emergers. Tiny, #20–24 Trico mayfly spentwings are big morning draws on most rivers. Small, #18–24 little blue-winged olive mayflies become a dominant species

Caddis emerger imitations are important to fishermen from early summer to late autumn, mostly in sizes #14–20.

Those big and ugly stonefly nymph imitations continue to fool big trout year in and year out. They work best just before, during, and after the salmon fly and golden stone hatches, which coincide with the higher-water period of late May to early July.

Nymphs in swift rivers tend to be a little bigger and wider than are many of those found in slow flows. The classic Hare's Ear Nymph plus the more recent Beadhead variation are excellent standbys in sizes #8–16.

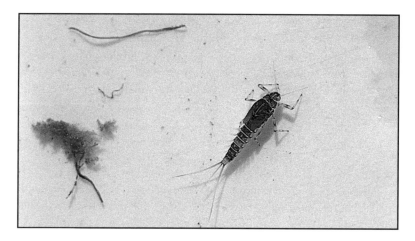

Slower-paced dam-controlled rivers feature high populations of smaller streamlined mayfly nymphs, mostly in the #16–22 size range. These need to be imitated closely for routine success.

toward the end of this period on some waters. The #14–18 *Callibaetis* mayflies, known as speckled-wing duns and spinners, are prominent lake mayflies and also show on slow, rich, and weedy rivers.

Many caddis species hatch now, most in sizes #14–22. Grays, tans, and browns are the most common wing colors, with bodies ranging from amber and tans to greens, grays, and browns. Bushy, high-floating patterns like Elkhair Caddis work well in most places. More realistic and slimmed-down feather-wing ties can be needed for pickier fish, especially when they are feeding on tiny naturals.

Ants, beetles, and grasshoppers figure more into the trout's diet from late July through September, too. On swift rivers with diverse hatches and light fishing pressure, attractor patterns, including Humpies, Trudes, Wulffs, and Stimulators, catch a lot of trout. These can be fished in smaller sizes as summer progresses, river levels bottom out, and trout become jaded. Hang a nymph from one for added action. On slower tailwater rivers, #16–22 flies can be needed routinely to match the small yet profusely hatching insects there. You can hang tiny nymphs from these, too.

SUBSURFACE EMERGERS

Emergers continue to be significant. Fishing pressure makes many trout a little surface-shy. Trout that started off taking dry flies freely can snub them now, preferring realistic emergers. Most important are PMD and caddis emergers down to #22 for picky bulging fish (a swirl, or bulge, appears on the surface but the fish are taking emergers just below it). Soft-hackles and Beadhead emergers work well, too, especially in swift runs and drop-offs. Check with a local fly shop to learn of the best current emerger patterns.

DEEP

Crayfish, sculpin, minnow, and leech patterns still produce some big fish. Beadhead mayfly nymphs and caddis pupae are top producers in broken freestone runs, swift channels, and the heads of pools: Beadhead Pheasant Tail Nymphs, Prince Nymphs, Serendipities, and Hare's Ears are prominent examples. Try going smaller if midsized patterns aren't doing the job. The majority of the midsummer hatches are smaller in size than those of spring.

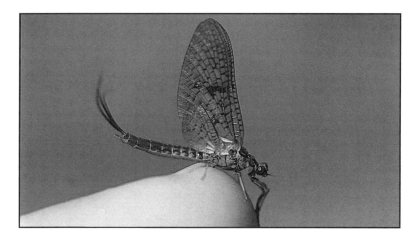

Brown drakes and green drakes are among the largest prominent western mayflies, in the #10–12 size range. These hatch mostly in late June to early July. Like most of the largest aquatic insect hatches, their seasonal duration is rather short. Ask around for your best local chances at such big fly–big fish encounters.

Tiny, #20–24 Trico mayfly spentwings (female egg layers that have died and fallen on the water) can coat rivers in late morning, with millions of them floating downstream. This occurrence goes on for two full months, from early July to mid-September in many cases. These insects will bring up lots of steady rising trout.

Cress bugs, scuds, San Juan Worms, and smaller Beadheads remain good tailwater bets. Minilarval imitations such as #18–24 Brassies make excellent droppers.

In some summer places "deep" means only a foot. In others it may mean 4–6 feet. Have plenty of leader-weighting and strike-indicator options, especially for midday, between hatch fishing. Hot, low-water summer days can find fish feeding languidly near the bottom (however deep) in the bright daylight hours.

Fall (October to November)

HATCHES

Little olive mayflies (*Baetis*) in #16–22 are most prominent. Parachutes, thorax ties, and Comparaduns are among the favorite pattern styles for this period. On some rivers, #14 mahogany duns, a rich brown mayfly, are present. Large, #12–14 white mayflies can hatch at dusk along slower silty-bottomed rivers in September and October.

Caddis continue, including the giant orange sedge, or October caddis. This rusty-orange-bodied, #8–10 monster of a caddis is prominent on many western rivers. Although the numbers aren't always high, the size begins getting the trouts' attention because hatches in general are becoming less diverse. Orange-bodied versions of Randall Kaufman's Stimulator are great searching patterns. They can also be used as strike indicators for nymph droppers. This combination has been a good fall producer for me before the afternoon hatches of *Baetis* mayflies kick in.

Hoppers continue working into early October, beetles and ants even later. Midges become very important in late autumn through winter as other hatches dwindle and give out for the season. Griffith's Gnats and midge pupae patterns will land many a fish. Hungry fall trout can pounce on attractor patterns between what hatches there are. Even on tailwater rivers, where picky fish are the rule, smaller H & L Variants, mini Royal Wulffs, and Parachute Adamses in #14–18 or even #20 will draw many a strike when fished blind. Rising trout in autumn seem less picky in general than they might have been a couple of months earlier. Where I fish, this is true.

On most rivers, big fish will always like some big flies. Crayfish patterns like this one aren't used much by anglers, but trout sure like the real thing!

SUBSURFACE EMERGERS

For pickier fish, #16–20 olive mayfly and #14–18 caddis emergers could be needed. A #18–22 midge pupa becomes more important as the season runs its course, especially on slower tailwater rivers. On swift backcountry rivers, #14–18 soft-hackle, regular, and Beadhead nymphs work well on hungry fall fish. These can be dead drifted or sunk, then lifted and swung in the current as an emerger. The generally lowering water temperatures after summer's heat extremes can invigorate autumn trout. Reckless feeding sprees are seen in some high-altitude trout when the water warms up a bit after an autumn night's chill. A couple hours of sunshine on the water can bring up the temperature enough to get them going. In some cases, almost any reasonable fly might work on them. This is my kind of fishing!

DEEP

The big stuff works well now. Egg patterns, too, are effective as we move into the brown trout and then the whitefish spawning seasons.

A #14–18 Beadhead Pheasant Tail Nymph is a killer prior to and during the day's afternoon *Baetis* mayfly hatches. Some superior

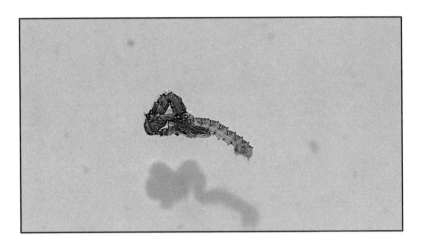

Tiny emerging midge pupae in sizes #18–24 make up a good percentage of an autumn and winter trout's diet. These are fished to rising and bulging fish, often as droppers trailing from tiny dry flies.

nymphing days may now be had. Cress bugs, Brassies, and the like remain tailwater mainstays. In freestone rivers, the same old Hare's Ears, Prince Nymphs, and the like will still be turning fish, Beadhead or not. Fall rivers are low, clear, and shallow. Their fish can be aggressive at times due to decreased availability of food. Spring rivers are nymph-rich, with many mature species ready to hatch. The opposite is the case in late fall, when nymphs are fewer, immature, and very small.

Moving into early winter, either small stuff or large naturals are most available to fish. Midge larvae and ascending pupae are most commonly on the small side, along with cress bugs and tiny nymphs. Midges hatch well all winter. Minnows, crayfish, and sculpins provide year-round fodder on the big end of the spectrum. Most of the medium-sized nymph and hatch options of spring and summer are unobtainable now. That doesn't mean a hungry fish won't eat a well-presented #14 Beadhead Hare's Ear, though. But with their lowered winter metabolism, trout are less likely to chase food down much of the day. It's better if it bounces off their noses! Egg and unrealistically bright-colored scud patterns (which are likely taken for eggs) can be top producers, too. These #12–18 flies are fished deep under indicators and can work well all winter.

This is the hatch scenario in a nutshell. Local hatches and their actual importance to your fishing will vary a great deal from river to river. Check with local fly shops and experts for hatch information pertinent to your fishing. Many of the patterns listed in the charts will work most places, though, during and between hatches. You can always slow-swim a Woolly Bugger, too, and gaze off at the scenery. Sometimes the no-brainer approach catches the biggest fish—like the 14-pound brown a kid yanked out of one of our local rivers while "Buggering" last summer!

INDEX

Aluminum boats, 140–141

Anchoring boats, 87–88, 99–100, 101, 109–114

Anchor systems, 148–151

Ants and beetles (hatches), 181, 192, 194

Aquatic insect hatches, 178–197; hatch charts, 179–182

Attractor fly patterns, 187, 192, 194

Baetis mayflies, 3, 179, 180, 182, 183, 184, 194, 195

Basic maneuvering, 20–34

Beadhead nymphs, 179, 182, 185, 187, 191, 192, 195

Bends, river, navigating and fishing, 40–41, 42, 70–72

Boat positioning, 107–114

Boat ramps, use of, 170–174; backing down, 172–174

Boat selection and rigging, 126–154; materials and, 138–145

Boat trailers. See Trailers, boat

Boulder gardens, 73–76

Boulders: collisions and, 52–60; flips and, 55–57; holes behind, 60–66

Bridges, rowing around, 74, 83–84, 90–91

Brown drake mayfly, 180, 187, 189, 193

Caddis, 179, 181, 182, 187, 188, 190, 192, 194

Callibaetis mayflies, 192

Camping, gear and preparation, 155–169

Casting, float fishing and, 107, 108–114, 115–123; reach cast, 110–111, 117–119, 122; skid cast, 122; tuck cast, 120–121; technique, 117–123

Catamarans, 128, 131

Crayfish, 179, 183, 192, 195

Cressbugs, 183, 194, 196

Diversion dams, 64, 66–67

Drift boats: 136–138, 139, 151–154; maneuvering, 20–34; eddies and, 33, 40–41, 75; side channels and, 42–44; obstacles, 27–34, 44–49

Drop-offs, fishing, 95, 105

Eddies, boats and, 33, 40–41, 75

Egg fly patterns, 195, 196

Emergers, 183, 187, 190, 192, 195, 196

Etiquette, floating, 171, 172, 174

Expedition rigging, 155–169

Ferrying, 16, 18, 25–31, 71–72

Fiberglass boats, 141–143

Float fishing. *See* Fly fishing, drift boats and
Floater's gates, 89
Fly fishing, drift boats and, 32–33, 40, 42–44, 76, 92–125
Fly patterns, 179–197. *See also* individual patterns

Glare, effects of, 88–89
Golden stonefly, 180, 186, 189, 190
Grasshoppers, 181, 192, 194
Green drake mayfly, 180, 187, 189

Hatches. *See* Aquatic insect hatches and individual insects
Hazards, river, 14–16, 18, 50–80; man-made, 89–91
High centering, rocks and, 35, 140
Holes (river hydraulics), 60–66
Horn oar locks, 6–8, 12
Hypothermia, 82–83

Island systems, fishing, 101–105

Launching, boat, 20–23, 28
Ledge drops, 66–67
Life jackets, 80
Lining, boats and, 76
Little blue-wing olive mayflies, 179, 180, 182, 184, 187, 189, 194
Little winter or black stoneflies, 179, 183, 184
Little summer stoneflies, 181, 189
Log jams, 67–70

Mahogany dun mayflies, 182, 194
Mayflies, 181, 187
Microcaddis, 181
Midges, 179, 182, 183, 187, 194, 196

Nymphs, 179–197

Oak blade angle, 6, 8, 12, 13

Oar holder, 154
Oar-lock designs, 6–11, 38; pin-and-clip, 7–9, 11, 12
Oar-lock stirrups, 7, 9, 11, 29
Oar rigging, 6–11, 38
Oar stoppers, 6, 7; oar right stopper, 8–9, 12
Oar stroke, basic, 5–6, 12–14
Oars, counter-balanced, 10; effective use of, 12–17; hand position on, 6; sweep, 36–37, 42–43
October caddis, 182, 194

Pale morning dun mayflies, 180, 187, 188, 189, 192
Permits, rivers and, 155, 160
Pink lady mayfly, 189
Pivot turns, 18, 20, 23–25, 37
Prams, 130, 133–136, 148–151

Rafts, 126–133, 134, 146–148, 155–156
Rapids, 73–84; scouting, 74–75; swimming/self-rescue in, 80–83
Reach casts. *See* Casting, float fishing and
Riffle corners, fishing, 95, 97–98
Rigging, boats, 145–154, 155–163
Rigging, oar, 7–10
River bends. *See* Bends, river, navigating and fishing
River gear, 124–125
River hazards. *See* Hazards, river
Rock gardens, 73–76
Rocker, in boats, 27, 29, 130, 133, 136
Rocks. *See* Boulders
Rods, 124–125
Ropes, 57–59
Rowing: basic stroke, 12–17; crawl stroke, 35–49; low water, 35, 48–49; obstacles (maneuvering around), 27–34, 44–49, 50–84; pace, 16; water depth and, 22, 29–30, 40–43; wind and, 29–31, 48, 85–88

Rowing gloves, 17
Rowing frames, raft, 132, 146–148

Salmonfly, 180, 187, 189, 190
Sculpin, 179, 186, 192
Self-bailing rafts, 77, 129, 155
Skid cast, 122
Shade, trout's use of, 3, 95, 106
Side channels, fishing, 95, 103–105
Slack-line casts, 110, 111, 119–120
Spring stoneflies, 179, 183
Stonefly nymphs, 179, 183, 186, 189, 190
Streamer flies, 179, 189
Subsurface emergers, 183, 187, 192
Summer stoneflies, 181, 189
Sweepers/strainers, 67–70

Tackle, float-fishing, 124–125
Tarps, 157–158, 161
Thunderstorms, rowing in, 86

Trailers, boats, 153
Trailering boats, 170–174
Trico mayflies, 181, 189, 193
Trout positions in rivers, 92–106
Tuck cast, 120–121
Two-fly rigs, 116, 117, 192, 194, 196

Wade fishing, 72, 86, 96, 97, 98, 100, 113
Waterproof bags and boxes, 159–160
Waves: 76–80; back-curling, 74, 76–79;
    compression, 74, 76–83; standing,
    76–80
Western march brown mayfly, 179, 183,
    185, 187
Whirlpools, 74, 83–84
White mayfly, 182, 194
Whitewater, 73–84
Wood boats, 143–145
Wrapped boats: boulders and, 51–60;
    freeing, 57–59